Stefan Esser
Riedel

Stefan Esser

Riedel

Glassmakers since 250 Years – History and Future

Translated from German by
Richard Manson,
Gordon H. Broxton-Price

DROEMER

www.riedel.com

Visit our website:
www.droemer.de

Original title of the German edition: Riedel. Glasmacher seit 250 Jahren – Geschichte und Zukunft.
Edited by: Jens Brandt (English language edition), Regina Carstensen (German language edition)
Jacket design: dasbauernhaus (der bauer Martin Kastner)
Jacket artwork: Thomas Schauer, Studio for Photography, Wien
Layout and production: Sandra Hacke
Reproduction: Repro Ludwig, A-Zell am See
Typesetting: Adobe InDesign by Droemer Knaur production department
Printing and binding: Appl OHG, Wemding
Printed in Germany
ISBN-13: 978-3-426-27384-5
ISBN-10: 3-426-27384-5

2   4   5   3   1

Contents

IV. The New Beginning:
Wineglasses with an Avant-garde Design

Appendix

Foreword

This book is not just the history of a company, but also of our family. Both have been closely connected for the last quarter of a millennium, so closely that today the one would not exist without the other. The two are inextricably linked and only together can they tell the Riedel success story.

The story begins in the second half of the 17th century with glass – and glass is also what links together events over the course of many wars and numerous crises. It may have received a few scratches in the process, but it has never shattered. To this day, glass bears testimony to our economic success and competence.

Eleven generations of Riedels can look back with pride at their success in the business. Until 1945, they lived in Northern Bohemia. Today they own several production sites in Austria and Germany. Their story vibrantly reflects each epoch.

It is an exciting stretch of history. No matter what year we might consider, 1700, 1800 or 2005, again and again it becomes clear that the future cannot be planned, and that chance moments and encounters lead to unexpected developments. And yet, hard work, discipline and intuition have always been our keys to survival.

It would seem that men have dominated the Riedel family history because up to now only men have led the company. Certainly, this may have been due to conservatism on occasion, but at other times it was a purely economic strategy. For there has always been only one priority, which goes before gender: The preservation of the company. Only one successor was ever supposed to decide the company's future in order to avoid any chance of the company splitting apart. However, no one could ever have acted without strong family backing. The role of women in the history of the Riedels can therefore not be emphasized strongly enough.

It would exceed the capacity of a single book to discuss every single member of the family. This business-*cum*-family-chronicle is restricted to the immediate proximity of the company. It stretches from 1678 to the death of Claus Riedel in 2004 – and beyond.

We would like to dedicate this book to the nine generations of Riedels who have gone before us – as well as to all the women of the dynasty, without whose understanding and support the successful survival of a family business would not have been possible.

In the tenth and eleventh generation:
Georg Riedel and Maximilian Riedel

The Leap to Freedom

It was March 16, 1946, a clear day. Groaning under the strain, the engine had fought its way up the long miles of the Brenner Pass, the long line of fully loaded wagons behind it not making it any easier. At an altitude of 1,370 meters, the tracks finally levelled out and the American train convoy stopped briefly at the border between Italy and Austria. The long trek then laboriously started again. On the Austrian side of the Brenner the going was downhill; it was steep with a lot of bends, forcing the engineer to drop the speed. In one of the cars at the rear where dozens of prisoners of war sat all over the place amongst the baggage, a slim figure of a man opened the rear exit door. It was unlocked, which was actually quite unusual. Most of the other German prisoners – once they had passed the border – had long since nodded off again. With the brakes screeching, the train very slowly approached a long, drawn-out bend.

Standing on the rusty iron steps, the young man glanced nervously to the left and right, then finally straight ahead. Here, directly behind the engine, was the wagon with the American guards and their heavy machine guns. Suddenly a narrow gap in the mountains appeared. This was his chance!

Flexing his knees several times, the 21-year-old took a deep breath, glanced to the front where the snow seemed much deeper than before, and then gave another concentrated look forwards to where the snorting and smoking engine was now swallowed up by the narrow bend in the line. The guards' wagon was about to disappear from view, too. It's now or never – nobody will be able to shoot at you here. The German prisoner of war ordered himself not to think of anything else. Jump – all that mattered now was to jump. A split second later, he was in free fall, to be caught by the icy cold in a billowing snow drift. He felt unpleasant wetness on his face, his body falling into a kind of stupor from fear of being seen. He lay motionless in the soft, crystalline whiteness, very much aware of the American officers sitting in the very last carriage who might still be a threat to him. Above him, frighteningly loud, the train's remaining carriages rumbled past. He dared not look up. Claus Riedel lay there as if paralyzed by so much courage and so much fear of being discovered by the Americans. When the rattling of the train had faded into the distance and peace and quiet had spread out all around him, he still did not dare to move.

Prisoner of war Riedel could hear his heart pounding out into the uncanny quiet. The more attention he paid to the sound of his pulse, the more intensely he also heard birds fluttering in the neighboring trees. All at once he was aware that he had escaped – that was it. This simple fact made him increasingly conscious of his surroundings, aware of the snow long melted on his cheek, the cold creeping through his tattered clothing and of the wetness on his arms and legs. What a marvelous feeling! Never before had cold and wetness felt so good. He was in Austria. He was no longer captive. Life might take an unexpected turn for the better after all.

Now Claus Riedel had to be careful that the Americans did not pick him up again. But where on earth should he go to? To Bohemia, his home? This

A leap – it was all he needed: Claus Riedel seized the opportunity to escape from a train and build himself a new future in Austria

was now no longer possible. That home did not exist any more. And yet the future now seemed wide open again: He had just been re-born.

He had ventured his escape during the train journey from Pisa to Bad Aibling in Upper Bavaria. There, the German prisoners were to be handed over to the French. What he had done in all uncertainty could not have been something he had planned. It had buzzed through his head again and again when, during the journey, he noticed that the carriage doors had not been locked – and the train would have to travel very slowly as it crossed the Alps. Off and on, he fell into a dazed state, the typical lethargy of prisoners of war. Nevertheless, he duly noted the unusually slack way the Americans dealt with their prisoners – probably the result of their feeling of superiority and the assumption that their main job was already done. They had ended

Lost homeland: The Riedel glassworks with their smokestacks in the Northern Bohemian town of Polaun (postcard around 1930)

World War II in their favor almost a year before – and he and the other German prisoners of war, who had spent the last few months in the camp at San Vincenzo in a pine forest on the coast of Tuscany, had been treated fairly.

Escape. During the monotonous rattling of the wheels, this idea had grown, taken possession of him more and more. *Escape. Why not?* He had to solve a thorny problem, *his* problem: The Riedel glass empire in northern Bohemia had been smashed after the end of the war and all family possessions confiscated by the Czechs. Despite all this, life for the Riedels had to go on somehow. *More time as a prisoner of war?* No, he was itching for something quite different. When the young man saw that both sides of the rail tracks at the top of the Brenner Pass were still well cushioned with thick snow, he only had to take this one risk ...

*

Claus Riedel's legendary leap at Berg Isel between the Brenner Pass and Innsbruck marked the turning point that led to the establishment of the present-day glass company Riedel in Kufstein. It was the start of what was to lead in the ensuing fifty years to the current position of Riedel as *the* wineglass company. Riedel has a worldwide reputation as the manufacturer of wineglasses of extremely fine quality and breathtaking, classic design. The company produces glasses that allow wines from a whole spectrum of different vines to fully develop their taste and reach their peak of enjoyment.

But Claus Riedel's leap to freedom has more than just symbolic power for today. The history of the Riedels goes back a quarter of a millennium, all the way to the middle of the 18th century. It is the history of a family dynasty which has defied all kinds of political collapse and economic crisis, in which artists and business people from eleven generations have dedicated themselves to the fascination of glass. – In doing so, they have had to make more than just one leap of faith.

*

Ranking amongst the most influential entrepreneurs in the European glass sector for centuries, the life of each Riedel generation was continuously closely interwoven with political, industrial and scientific events. Their family history reads like a thrilling reflection of each period concerned, making it more alive, more tangible. The Riedels belong to one of the oldest houses in the art of glassmaking with a tradition that has never been interrupted for very long. It sounds almost like a fairy tale; and reminds us maybe of a pleasantly light and sweet wine. In truth, these almost uninterrupted 250 years in the glass-making trade were only possible because each generation went about

their business with a passion. They did not give up in difficult times and felt not only committed to personal and economic success, but also to the well-being of their own families and the people working for them. The saying is still true today for any Riedel glassmaker: »The furnace must burn on«. Those who know Georg Riedel – representing the tenth generation – have learned what this family understands by entrepreneurship: You need »punch«, forever applying your creative verve to go on developing the company with optimism, discipline and love.

Each Riedel generation has been faced by its own set of problems and has dealt with them almost invariably with bravura. The present tenth and eleventh generation – Georg Riedel's son Maximilian already has an executive position in the USA business – are now delivering more and more Riedel glasses to the lovers and connoisseurs of good wine around the world. Today they are working under completely different circumstances than those encountered by Johann Leopold Riedel, who, in 1756, by starting his own glassworks in the forests of Northern Bohemia, laid the cornerstone for two and a half centuries of glass manufacturing under the name of one family. Nevertheless, the challenges do remain similar to a certain degree – this is borne out by such a long family tradition. In a globalized world, it is important to have good strategic planning– together with a little bit of luck and great personal involvement. But wasn't it like that for Johann Leopold Riedel as well? After all, he started with his glassworks right in the middle of an economic depression – and was successful nonetheless.

The writer Hans Kruppa once quipped, »Truly

Cup vase from 1936 engraved with the family tree of Josef Riedel junior (1862–1924) and his wife Paula.
Inscription: *For our mother and grandmother on her 70th birthday*

ich is he who dreams more than reality can destroy.« Erich Kästner said, »You can also build something beautiful from the stones that are placed in your way.« And finally it was Johann Wolfgang von Goethe who noted, »What you inherit from your fathers must be earned before it can be truly yours.« To follow the Riedels' exciting history is to see how well these three quotations fit this family of entrepreneurs– as if the writers had been thinking of them.

It is important to have a mere moneymaking, not to times, and to feel responsi one has been entrusted. T been the mark of the Rie tions.

The family has always innovation. They have alw ing – Claus Riedel's leap fr of this tradition.

The »Riedel Original« and his Grandson's First Glass Factory

Pushing a Handcart through the Debris of the Thirty Years War

The decades of the Thirty Years War rank among the darkest and hardest times ever to have cast their shadow over Europe, yet the years that followed as the Riedel dynasty sought its beginnings were equally challenging.

The Thirty Years War started as a religious conflict and ended as a clash between European powers. Such protracted wars meant that the military coffers were frequently empty. The result of this was that killing, pillaging and marauding were the order of the day. Whole countries, towns and cities were laid to waste, and people tended to become lethargic. In many regions, people's lives were reduced to a passive, monotonous existence. Fighting for sheer survival after years of fear and destitution, they were no longer interested in contests for political power between provincial princes and the imperial power base, nor in confessional disagreements between the Catholic League and Protestant Union.

Starvation and barbarism, plundering, rape and the senseless slaughtering of civilians held sway from Westphalia to Bohemia. When the news of enemy soldiers closing in – be they Swedes or mercenaries – whose origins the people were not even aware of, was carried to the villages by word of mouth, the locals lived in fear that they would no longer see the next sunrise.

Peace resolutions – such as Lübeck in 1629 or Prague in 1635 – turned into a farce, since they were soon flouted, battles enflaming anew. The French took their bloody trail right up to Bavaria, and the Swedes invaded Bohemia, which had already suffered terribly with summary trials, massacres and epidemics. Finally they stood at the gates of Prague. Albrecht von Wallenstein, who as imperial commander was supposed to stop the Swedes, had long since been murdered by them; the imperial Bavarian-Spanish troops had towards the end almost only been on the defensive. As opponents of the emperor, the Franconians seized the moment and openly went over to the Swedes.

The emperor had to yield: Interminable negotiations finally put an end to the slaughter which had cost the lives of over a third of the population in the areas where the war had been fought. On October 24, 1648, the Peace of Westphalia was concluded. Europe was left hardly able to breathe.

And yet before the war, a good number of people had fared rather well, such as in Bohemia, where the numerous glassmakers in the forests – in those days huge quantities of wood were needed as fuel to produce this material– had built up a flourishing trade. The first written records of a glassworks come from the 16th century. One, run by a glassmaker named Paul Schierer, existed in Reiditz (today Rejdice), and was operational during the rule of Jaroslaus von Smirecky. This is verified by a document with the notation »de dato Wednesday after St. Hieronymus anno 1577«. Even in those early days of glass production, a Protestant priest in Joachimsthal wrote of decisive changes in daily life,

of new drinking habits, »offensively big glasses«
and »ghastly boozing«.

Other documents, such as one from around
1900 – it is kept in the state archives in Bohemian
Gablonz (today Jablonec) – impressively illustrate
the later decline of the glassmakers' art in the Bohemian region. According to this document everything was quite in order for the glassmakers there
before the fighting broke out. True, they did not
have any land or property of their own, since it
belonged to the »glassworks master«. The glassmakers were thus tenants on his land, but they still
earned more than enough. This relative prosperity
came to an end in the period from 1618 to 1648.
How this came about is described in the Gablonz
archives based on the house records of the glassworks master Bartholomäus Schürer von Waldheim,
where incidentally, as in many documents from this
period, reference is made to the »disease of the
head«, which we know today as encephalitis:
»Anno 1635, December and Advent, I moved with
wife and children to Reichenberg because of the
great threat of war, robbery, pestilence and the
danger of the head disease; stayed a good 20 weeks.
There, too, the disease of the head broke out, and I
suffered from it a number of weeks. On the 3rd Advent I went to Grünwald and visited my plundered
house and apartment. The illness set in at the Grünwald fair and I suffered terribly. May God watch
over each and every devout Christian!« But his
hope wasn't fulfilled. A little later, his wife gave
birth to a daughter, who died of malnutrition shortly afterwards because the mother suffered from an
epidemic disease and could not nurse the child.

When at last the dreadful wave of killing, starvation and deprivation was contained, the people

Hollow glassworks with furnace and glass blowers in Hohberg
(copper engraving from 1687)

were left distraught in their devastated villages and
towns. Nobody believed in a future – since in fact
new skirmishes were still constantly taking place.
Robbers and highwaymen made travel and trade
routes unsafe for decades to come. Any hint of
humanity had been sacrificed to brutal cruelty. One
must bear this in mind in order to comprehend the
achievements of those people who did not give up
in the face of such adversity. Anyone wanting to
pull themselves out of the squalor of ruin amid this
agony had to be daring, tough and full of optimism,
they had to believe in themselves and not in the
opinions generally voiced by others.

Particularly intrepid after the Peace of West-

Setbacks for the Bohemian glass industry: Arson and massacres by marauding troops in the Thirty Years War (painting by Karel Svoboda, after the Battle of White Mountain, 1620)

One glassworks after another was built in this densely wooded region. The products manufactured by the glassmakers were carefully packed for the glass dealers, who would come and buy from the glassworks and then, heavily laden, trade their wares throughout the countryside. After the devastation of war, the glass traders had no problems with sales – the drinking glasses and glass tankards provided people with a little *joie de vivre*. Moreover, the traders almost always took along any number of bull's-eye panes with them, there hardly being any house after this seemingly eternal war in which no window had been broken.

Each of the glass traders was left to his own devices. He would lug as many wares as he could carry. Dealer networks and trading posts did not exist – let alone logistics in a Europe that the war had practically catapulted back to the Stone Age.

But there were a host of competitors. While the glass industry in Northern Bohemia was only just starting, it had long been established in Vienna, in Tyrol and in the Spessart region. It took some decades before the glassmakers and glass traders from Northern Bohemia – mostly German immigrants from the north and northeast through the Jizera and Sudeten Mountains, who settled in the former Slavic territory – were able to hold their

phalia were the dealers and craftsmen who, with their barrows and carts, had to leave the more or less securely enclosed villages and cities to venture through the countryside to the next towns. At this time, the scissor grinders reported to the villagers and townspeople that the briskest business was currently being done with glass. Objects made of this material were readily presented in parlors to testify to a family's prosperity. And so it was: People with money would surround themselves with glass bowls, wine glasses – and new window panes.

At that time, great quantities of glass were manufactured close to the Bohemian hamlet of Gablonz.

own in the European markets. They managed this only with great tenacity and flexibility and supreme physical effort. Many traders had another source of income other than glass. They ground knives and scissors, worked glass parts with their cutting tools to meet their customers' wishes or sold fabrics, particularly the popular Bohemian linen. What should not be forgotten is that the Bohemian dealers were stubborn, relying on what we would nowadays call »power selling«. In Leipzig, for example, they drove the glassmakers' guild to despair.

In a petition to the city, the guild complained that »quite a few farmhands and such from Bohemia [...] bring in many cases of glass not just to market, but between the markets, peddling in lanes and cellars throughout the whole year, and so snatching the very bread from our mouths«. By 1690, traders who could afford it started to use small horse carts instead of pushcarts and wheelbarrows.

The job was hard. They had to do their business in summer to be back home in time before the hard winter set in, in order to prepare glass for the next season, work it and get everything ready for the months of travel and travail. But the work did bring success and money; a growing number of traders made their long way from northern Bohemia's remote forests to Russia, Constantinople, to the Baltic and as far as London, since nearby markets were soon saturated. In the Bohemian community Steinschönau (today Kamenicky Senov), for example, of the 73 house owners, 34 worked as glass dealers in 1713.

Traveling as a glass merchant in the mountains meant enduring many dangers – even giants (Liebig trading card from 1898)

The Worldwide Success of Bohemian Glass

The major upswing that Bohemian glass was set to enjoy at the end of the 17th century resulted from the development of the new chalk crystal glass. It replaced the old greenish forest glass that was characterized by a certain coarseness. On the other hand, the solid, thick-walled chalk crystal glasses ideal for surface and deep cut (or intaglio) engraving suited the new Baroque taste better than the thin-walled Renaissance forms of Venetian glasses. Because of this, Venice tried to fend off Bohemian glass with import embargos as early as at the beginning of the 18th century – about the time we also encounter the first-generation Riedel, Johann Christoph Riedel. The glass traders were able to overcome this embargo, since they had long extended their business contacts over the entire European continent. They were riding on a wave of success. One dealer reported he had brought »many hundreds of thousands of glasses« to Moscow and sent 20,000 glasses to a merchant in Southern Spanish Cadiz, who shortly thereafter placed a repeat order for the same amount. Spain in general turned into an especially good market for Bohemian glass in the 18th century: In 1714, the War of Succession had come to an end, wood was in short supply in Spain, which had hardly any glassworks of its own, and the import duties were low. On the other hand, the gigantic flow of gold and silver from its colonies had made Spain rich. What is more, Spain was a trading nation doing business with America and India. The city of Cadiz enjoyed an export monopoly for the American colonies. Here, small Spanish merchants were active as intermediaries, and glassware from

Bohemian dealers was often for sale in its covered streets.

The seafaring power of Portugal also boosted the Bohemian economic miracle. In 1715, fourteen dealers from the Bohemian forests joined forces to form a »Confederation and Association«. With this network, they wanted to protect themselves against certain questionable business practices employed by various small merchants. The Bohemian glass traders went about this very skillfully. According to an old document, the glass trade with the entire Iberian Peninsula »has met with such a reception that almost every honest tradesman has completed his journey contented and returned with satisfying money, with which both the distributor and the glass worker were well paid. Therefore with one thing and another a pretty penny has come to stay in the fatherland«.

A later report noted: »It is said that they had sold the glass at enormous profit within a short time, so that our glass negotiators soon developed lively activities in other Spanish harbors as well, and in up-river Seville that had great importance for home trade«.

It was in those days of the Bohemian glass boom, at the beginning of the 18th century, that the first in the Riedel dynasty, Johann Christoph Riedel, tried his luck. It was a period when, within a few short years, the entire coastland of the European continent was gradually dotted with Bohemian branches of the glass trade, for individual dealers were unable to cope with the rapidly growing demand. Classic bartering was constantly engaged in as well, which meant that the Russians paid for the

Shards of glass from the Karlshütte works in the Jizera mountains (1758–1775). They were found in archaeological digs in the 1970s at the former works location

glassware with furs, the Spaniards with tobacco. In following decades there were occasional economic setbacks, sometimes caused by a drop in demand and sometimes by political circumstances – Johann Leopold Riedel, the third of the dynasty and the company founder, experienced this in 1752 right at the beginning of his career. However, despite these various crises, the market grew to an extent which could never have been anticipated. One Bohemian trading company, for example, supplied 11,500 cases and barrels with glass products to its Spanish branches between 1775 and 1825. In 1792 alone, this trading company had purchased one million unworked glasses in Northern Bohemian glassworks, then processed and packed them in crates weighing up to 1,600 pounds.

The glass business was not easy, traders had to overcome many adversities on their travels. The important port of Hamburg, for example, could only be reached from Northern Bohemia by land. Fortunately, there were large wagons, which when loaded had to be drawn by six to eight horses. Saxony, in turn, prohibited the Bohemian merchants from trading on the Elbe River by ship, presumably because August I of Saxony, luxury and power-oriented as he was, was obliged by the road toll franchises to direct Bohemian trade overland.

Child labor was the norm in those days, not only in the Northern Bohemian glassworks. The explosion in trade demanded a large workforce. Many young boys were sent to work at the trading outposts at ten and eleven years of age. It was the norm for these small fellows to walk their way right across Europe, few having the means to ride by stagecoach. In the settlements, they started in the warehouse, and in many instances they were then made messengers. Really bright lads could work their way into the commercial side. They were only allowed out accompanied by an adult. Attending fairs was mandatory and anyone who did not obey was sent back to Bohemia, which was considered the greatest disgrace. By the time a trade trainee could be considered a partner and allowed to marry, he was often already around forty.

The Bohemian glass business experienced further setbacks with the American Wars of Independence: In the French and Indian War (the American theater of the Seven Years War of 1756–1763) the English-speaking colonies in America loosened the grip of the French, who had been in a territory-sharing pact with Spain, and in the War of Independence (1775–1783) they seceded from the British motherland. For much of this war, the English had occupied and blockaded American harbors on the east coast. In Europe this also led to much tension between Spain, England and France. These wars paved the way for the founding of the United States, but the Bohemian glassmakers and traders got the short straw: Glass exports to distant countries and direct trade with Spain almost came to a halt, but new avenues were invariably found. They started, for example, to produce ornamental glass for local markets. Nevertheless, at the beginning of the 19th century, another acute economic disaster hit the glass-land of Northern Bohemia. This resulted from Napoleon's Russian campaign. Only after 1813, when Napoleon suffered a devastating defeat at Leipzig, were the people in Europe able to hope for better times. In good times, the glass manufacturers and traders usually earned exceptionally well, in bad times they muddled through as best they could. One of these early traders was Johann Christoph Riedel. At the beginning of the 16th century, he journeyed through the countryside as a glass trader – and sometimes when he had sold well he returned laden with coins.

This, however, proved to be his undoing.

Many glass beads from the Riedel works had a long journey ahead. An African woman with glass bead jewelry (oil painting by Albert Eckhout, 1641)

As in Schiller's Ballad »The Cranes of Ibycus«: The Murder Most Foul of the »Riedel Original«

One of the ethnic German Bohemian traders who, at the beginning of the 18th century, did not shy from the long and exhausting journeys fraught with danger and privation was a tough old German by the name of Johann Christoph Riedel. This glass trader from Neuschloss near Bohemian Leipa (today Jezve near Lipa), traveling with his wares through Europe, did not found the present-day glass company. That story did not begin until 1756 when the first glassworks operated as a free enterprise. He was, however, the father of all the Riedels and had almost the same affinity for glass as his descendants. His own dramatic, indeed horrific, life story shows how quickly outrageous fortune can change everything, even in the life of a successful man. The Riedel family history reflects the ups and downs of historical, social, technical and political developments over the decades and centuries – probably because the individual family members, among other things, were invariably ahead in their field. Certainly, they enjoyed some good fortune and also had the best of opportunities, but they required a great deal of staying power and creativity to utilize these advantages. Again and again, there were situations when carrying on seemed nigh on impossible. Confronted by possible ruin, even more staying power was needed.

Johann Christoph Riedel, however, found himself in a situation where he had no chance: He was murdered. As the story goes, his death occurred in 1723 in Markersdorf (today Markvartice) near Kamnitz (today Kamenice on the tributary to the Jizera River of the same name). It was handed down as a legend, recorded by Anton Paudler in his work *Ein deutsches Buch aus Böhmen* (»A German Book from Bohemia«) in 1895. Friedrich Schiller wrote his famous ballad *Die Kraniche des Ibykus* (»The Cranes of Ibycus« – 1797) years after Johann Christoph Riedel's violent death, reminding us so much of the legend of the glass trader Riedel that one inevitably wonders whether Schiller was inspired by it. Only the setting is different: Schiller's Ibycus is murdered in Poseidon's spruce grove near Corinth.

According to Paudler's legend, Johann Christoph Riedel was *en route* from a business trip in the Holy Roman Empire and Poland to the wedding of a cousin in Markersdorf. But he never arrived. Instead, he was discovered murdered »in the dense woods« of the Rosendorf Forest near there. Two brothers, scoundrels to be sure, who knew that he often returned from his travels with lots of money, had waylaid him as he merrily strode through the undergrowth.

> And on he hastes, in joyous mood,
> And reaches soon the middle wood
> When, on a narrow bridge, by force,
> Two murderers sudden bar his course.
> He must prepare him for the fray,
> But soon his wearied hand sinks low;
> Inured the gentle lyre to play,
> It ne'er has strung the deadly bow.

This is how Schiller (translation anon. 1902) in his ballad describes the death of the singer Iby-

Friedrich Schiller wrote his ballad *The Cranes of Ibycus* based on a legend that tells of the murder of the glass merchant Johann Christoph Riedel (copper engraving from 1873)

Sächs. Böhm. Schweiz. Eingang zur Klamm

A valley on the Kamnitz: On a little bridge on the Kamnitz, Johann Leopold Riedel decided to continue his glassworks (postcard around 1910)

cus, who had been accompanied for a while by cranes:

> *Deep-wounded, down he sinks at last,*
> *When, lo! the cranes' wings rustle past.*
> *He hears, – though he no more can see,*
> *Their voices screaming fearfully.*

Ibycus, facing death and despairing that nobody would hear of the crime inflicted on him, cried out:

> *By you, ye cranes, that soar on high,*
> *If not another voice is heard,*
> *Be borne to heaven my murder-cry!*
> *This he cries out, as his eye »breaks«.*

The legend of the murder of glass trader Riedel relates that two crows flew over the forest cawing loudly when the thieves were bludgeoning their victim. At this moment, the trader is said to have pleaded, »Let me live, I have no money on me, may the crows bear me witness.« The murderers did not spare him but found only half a *kreuzer* as booty. After finishing their deed, they went back to the new tavern in Markersdorf to take part in the wedding celebrations without compunction. Then the two crows, cawing loudly, came flying over the courtyard where one murderer said to the other: »Listen, those are Riedel's witnesses.« Guests sitting near the villains heard these words by chance. Moreover, they noticed traces of blood on the one brother's shirt, leading them to take the two possible culprits into provisional custody. A search was organized for Johann Christoph Riedel who had already been missed. Soon the wedding guests discovered his corpse in the forest – and his butter box. Under the butter, they found the ducats

he had earned on his trading travels. The two criminals were executed in Markersdorf.

In Schiller's ballad, the murderers also return after their deed to the festivities where the victim was headed, a singers' competition in Corinth. And here, too, the birds, an army of cranes, circle over the party, crying loudly, and one of the murderers shouts:

> *See there, see there, Timotheus!*
> *Behold the cranes of Ibycus!*

It was clear to all that the missing Ibycus had been killed by a murderer's hand. The culprits were subsequently arrested and received their just sentence:

> *The scene becomes the tribunal;*
> *Their crimes the villains both avow,*
> *When 'neath the vengeance stroke they fall.*

The Bohemian account of Johann Christoph Riedel, passed on by word of mouth right down to the 20th century, is in part – with regard to the murderers' execution – recorded in Schiller's treatise *Topographie von Böhmen* (»The Topography of Bohemia« – 1787). This is a clear indication of the inspiration for the ballad he wrote ten years later. It also provides evidence against the view that it was perhaps the other way around, that Schiller thought up his Ibycus purely on the basis of Greek mythology and that the people in Bohemia had »enhanced the status« of Riedel's death afterwards through the ballad's lasting impression. Even this version of events can be considered an honor for the »Ur-Riedel« as he has come to be known in German – the Riedel Original, the Very First Riedel. Either way, Schiller certainly knew the tale before he wrote his ballad.

May 17, 1756:
The Birth of the Riedel Glassmaking Enterprise

The murdered Johann Christoph Riedel had three sons: Johann Carl (1701), Johann Christoph (1706) and Jeremias (1709). Johann Carl, the first-born, followed in his father's footsteps to a certain extent – he also was an enthusiast for glass – rather less for the hazardous journeys that proved to be his father's downfall. As the second of the eleven generations of the Riedel family, Johann Carl learned how to produce glass. It turned out that he had real artistic talent, and he became a gilder and glass painter in Bohemian Falkenau (today Falknov). He then relocated with his wife Anna Elisabeth to the earlier glassworks of Bartholomäus Schürer, and finally, in 1739, was appointed judge in his community by the local authority. At that time, the Riedels lived under the rule of the city of Kamnitz. Johann Carl and his wife led the lives of upright citizens, and brought nineteen children into the world, seventeen of whom died at an early age. There is not much more known about this particular ancestor but rather more about his son, third in the dynastic succession. Born in 1726, Johann Leopold became the founder proper of the actual glass manufacturing company.

Johann Leopold was a Riedel like the entrepreneurs of this name we know today: He was tough, goal-oriented and always looking for new challenges. He learned glass painting from his father and when he was twenty, his cousin Johann Kittel took him on as a works clerk in the prestigious old Falkenau glassworks. Everything worked out for the best. Just a little later in 1752, Johann Leopold was able to move up the career ladder, by way of his cousin, as the administrator in the Zenkner glassworks in the hamlet of Antoniwald (today Antoninov) in Josephstal (today Josefuv Dul). Riedel proved himself to be reliable and highly talented at glass production.

Yet a lack of self-confidence almost led to his name becoming a mere footnote in the history of glassmaking in Northern Bohemia. Johann Leopold Riedel had started glassmaking in these works in an economically difficult period. Glass prices fell daily, the sales and volume figures hit rock bottom, and the young businessman did not have any large savings. Due to these general problems, his cousin had to stop operations in his own works, meaning he could not help either. It was a desperate situation.

Johann Leopold
Riedel
(1726–1800)

Glassmaster Riedel wanted to struggle against these economic difficulties together with his talented assistant Johann Joseph Dressler, but he just did not know on what front he should do battle. Why manufacture glassware when there were no longer any customers in sight? Everything seemed hopeless in this crisis. Finally, Riedel decided that his only possibility was to leave this place of failure quietly. He allowed the furnace to grow cold, bundled up his things, closed the glassworks door behind him and set out into an uncertain future.

He did not get a hundred paces. In front of the works, a small bridge crossed the Kamnice where he happened to meet his glassmaker Johann Dressler, who looked askance at this man prepared for travel. Johann Leopold Riedel was embarrassed by the situation, sneaking away from the region like this, but what else was he supposed to do? He told Dressler his reasons for leaving. Dressler listened to him quietly, but once he had heard the explanations, he simply said, »I think you've made too rash a decision. Even when we see no help is forthcoming, God can still give us succor. Trust Him, and it will be He who will show you the ways and means for you to get out of this sad situation.«

Riedel was touched by the optimistic nature of his assistant and returned home with a feeling of hope to rethink his situation again in peace and quiet and faith in God. Indeed, a thought came to him he had not considered up till now: He was a good acquaintance of Czerny, the magistrate of Morchenstern (today Smrzovka), and Czerny liked him, which Riedel knew; he simply would have to describe to him candidly the situation as it was and ask him for help. As expected, Czerny was under-

»The Interior of a Glassworks« (etching based on a drawing by Daniel Chodowiecki, 1774)

standing and said that if no other friend could help him, »I have 500 florins just lying around here. You will accept them as a small, interest-free loan until your business is in order and you are in a position to return them to me.« Riedel returned to his works again highly motivated, and it did not take long for the general economic situation to take a turn for the better. Just one year later, in 1753, the outstanding glassmaker Johann Leopold was able to pay the loan back to Czerny.

Riedel's successful work led to him becoming the first glass entrepreneur in the Riedel family on May 17, 1756. Due to his successful work, Count Karl Josef Desfours gave him written permission to run independently under lease, the Zenkner glassworks that was part of the Desfours Morchenstern estate. The first Riedel glass production had started.

»Witnessed this year A.D. 1756«:
The Young Entrepreneur Riedel Acquires a Lease

The lease granted by Count Carl Josef Desfours (different spellings of his name are passed down) to Johann Leopold Riedel, written in the old German script with thick strokes of the pen and hardly legible for us today, bears an imposing seal, authenticating the first independent Riedel glass enterprise. Today, it hangs enlarged and framed in the company's offices in Kufstein. With this lease agreement, the thirty-year-old Johann Leopold was to found an international family-owned enterprise. The content was as follows:

This day, of the year and date written below, by my benevolent permission within the power of my Gross-Rohosetz and Morchenstern privilege, with discretion and deliberation has been verily decreed this contract for 3 years establishing for Johann Leopold Riedel, born in Falkenau, the stewardship of the glassworks in Antoniwald and the adjoining estate fields and meadows and the steward's farm buildings and other properties. To wit:

He leases a title for business within the high county Gross-Rohosetz for the glassworks in Antoniwald belonging to the Morchenstern manor including the accompanying manor fields and meadows and their unplowed edges and markers, such as they have always been designated, and in the way and with the permission he himself in the past was able to enjoy, to Johann Leopold Riedel for 3 years from the 1st of January of the coming year under both of the following written obligations, they being:

1. The obligation that the lessor of the business title in the county of Gross-Rohosetz set aside for the above-mentioned lessee such firewood from the manor forests as is necessary for the continuous firing of the glassworks furnaces for at least 40 weeks throughout the year, however with the condition that officers from the manor and forestry authorities will be present each time for measurements and that the forest and tree-felling regulations are to be obeyed exactly according to their required guidelines so that trunks and boughs are not chopped irregularly but rather in clearly defined areas and that continuously from year to year the new growth of that wood can be managed and in turn brought to the best possible growth. It shall be permitted that in those distant forests which are so difficult to access the lessee shall receive a felling right to secure at his own labor costs a sufficient supply of 2,200 barrels of 2 cubit-long firewood such that the necessary amount of dried, thick wood and kindling can be felled and gathered in the presence of the manor and forestry officer without additional monies paid to the woodsman of the forestry office. That the lessee shall be obliged to secure and transport such thick, cleared lumber and kindling wood likewise at his own cost without causing competition for the benevolent

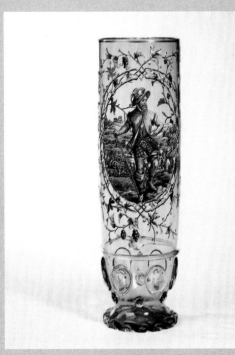

A tankard for thirsty mouths: Green glass in bright enamel colors, painted with a pilgrim. Made in the Josef Riedel enhancement works in 1886

forest authority or its workers throughout the year.
As regards

2. felled and standing beech wood, the ashes of which the lessee requires for glass materials, so shall the manor and forestry offices designate and *sub speciali reservati* set aside from the coming wood markets for the lessee a befittingly required amount for his indispensable need at market prices, as a result of which said lessee, barring windfall in the forests, is to be presented with no fresh wood nor is to fell it.

3. The lessee remains beholden that he shall fill the chambers for maintaining his furnaces with the sand which is required in the glassworks for the mixing of its materials by his own means and without assistance from the estate workers and without competing with the manor authority.
No less so

4. is the lessee alone responsible for quarrying, procuring and transferring to the glassworks the grates or appliances, stoking stones, necessary for preventing the furnaces from extinguishing, with the advantage, however, that the lessee at appropriate times and without disturbance of the administrative or manor offices may engage laborers from the estate as is befitting, and pay them a transport fee in coin. The Rohosetz manor office is not nor will be prepared to reimburse him for this purpose. In addition

5. the lessee shall be permitted to conduct free trade and commerce for the needs of his own family and servants or glassworkers or other employees for clothing, comestibles and food , with the exception of beer and salt materials. Notwithstanding,

6. the lessee is expressly required and obliged to procure for the needs of his glassworks throughout the year all he requires for the people and all that is necessary for keeping the beer on draught, measured at 4 buckets for each keg of beer, from the Morchenstern manor brewery, to pour and offer same with-

out adding his own contents and shall be required to pay in full and good amount for each keg the common current price in addition to a tap deposit of 24 kr. to the Morchenstern coffers. Similarly

7. the lessee agrees to take into the works as much brandy as can be required annually from the Morchenstern manor brandy distiller according to this binding contract and to sell it with the indubitable attestation of the Rohosetz manor management office that the Morchenstern manor brandy distiller shall at all times supply him with satisfactory, palatable brandy. However, insofar as

8. the lessee is required to account for his crates and other wood at his own expense and cost as described above in sub-point 1, the lessee pledges herewith firstly to pay a transport fee of 7 kr. for each bundle and secondly to secure a sufficient supply from year to year for 40 weeks and longer if possible and, should material be added to such wood by the manor laborers, to pay a fee for this in addition to the rent. No less

9. shall the glassworks' tenant be obliged and liable with all his property and goods to render annually 500 guilders in rent to the Morchenstern estate. Whether he engages in glasswork for a longer or shorter time or follows another pursuit or at times slackens, he is to pay in current coinage and in full. And

10. because the same is obliged by all means to maintain the iron machinery in the inventory of the glassworks in a good and useful condition, should upon return there be anything damaged, the repair of which would mean expense for the estate authority, he is subsequently to assume the repair at his own cost in order to bring it into a useful condition and return it to its previous state. So that in the future it may be used and enjoyed. Likewise

11. all of those fallow and arable fields and meadows belonging to the steward's farm are granted the tenant for his pleasure by the manor and forestry office for an additional interest of 61 fl. 24 kr. Adjacently

12. the glassworks, rooms, stalls, barn and a cellar shall be provided to the works tenant for his humble use. No less

13. shall he be permitted to keep and graze as much working, dairy and beef cattle as he is able, insofar as it causes no damage to the forests and wildlife beyond the areas allowed for pasture.

14. He will in the future be responsible for repairs to the living quarters, whereby the necessary building supplies are to be purchased through the manor office without compensation. In conclusion,

15. that within the terms of this lease, the benevolent estate authority may be insured and

that the described obligations and conditions may be observed with certainty by the lessee both in the use of labor and of other services, whatever they be named, not covered by this payment, the lessee shall be obliged to submit a written deposit of 500 guilders, and shall at all times conduct himself properly.

To confirm and record the contents of this contract, it has been written in two identical copies and witnessed and signed by hand by both negotiating parties next to the seal. One copy will be left in the possession of the Gross-Rohosetz estate office, the other with the lessee of the glassworks.

Witnessed this day in Gross-Rohosetz, December 31, 1755

LS Franz W. Chalaupka
pT Manor Director

LS Joh. Josef Grim
pT Administrator

LS Johann Leopold Riedel
Glass Master

This agreed contract is hereby confirmed by God's grace. Witnessed this day at Gross-Rohosetz Palace, May 17 in the year of 1756 Karl Josef Defours

The Riedel glass enterprise expands:
The Zenkner works in Antoniwald is no longer
a little forest hut

Famine, a Town of Broken Windows and a Letter of Release from the Prince

The Count naturally had to ensure his dues and conditions contractually, but he never had to regret leasing the glassworks to the young entrepreneur Riedel. Johann Leopold Riedel held a course bound for success and expansion, in which the Seven Years' War was inadvertently beneficial to him. This war started in the same year as Riedel established his company – in 1756.

After the seven years of fighting, in which Prussia and England fought against Austria, France, Russia and Sweden, towns and villages were frequently no more than mere heaps of rubble. When France and Russia left the Austrian alliance, Austria – financially in ruins – had no choice but to offer peace negotiations. On February 15, 1763, the Peace of Hubertusburg put an end to the war that had left behind unbelievable devastation. In Zittau, not far from Johann Leopold Riedel's glassworks, practically every window pane in the town lay shattered. Towards the end of the war, the Austrians had demanded the surrender of the city of Zittau by the Prussians, but met with no reaction, the Austrians went into a fury. They bombarded Zittau to such an extent that almost all the windows in the town were smashed. Empress Maria Theresia donated 50,000 guldens for the city's reconstruction »in special appreciation of courage«. The holes in the city's walls resulted in a gap in the market for glass, a need for glassmakers – but particularly for Johann Leopold Riedel. Only he was capable of producing especially clear and qualitatively good window panes in a size that other glass-works were unable to manufacture: Whereas the others still followed their fathers' ways, producing small, light-swallowing bulls-eye windows , Riedel was already supplying proper one-piece panes. He made them by blowing large glass bulbs, cutting them open and rolling them flat.

The ghastly scale of the war's ravages and the duration of the subsequent reconstruction can be gathered from Johann Leopold Riedel's order books from that time: For almost twenty years, he continued to supply great quantities of window panes to the Zittau master glazier Christoph Lennert. Notwithstanding this, Riedel's drinking vessels, glassware in hollow form, were being delivered to more and more distant regions, with leading local glass traders complaining to their rulers about this unpleasant competition. A report of the German Mountain Society written in 1927 had the following to say about this period:

Riedel understood how to adapt his production of unworked glass to the up-and-coming Gablonz glass industry specializing in small articles of merchandise, while at the same time not neglecting the manufacture of both hollow glass and flat panes. By doing so he not only promoted the development of the Gablonz glass industry, but practically secured its continued existence.

Now all was well with Johann Leopold Riedel, his Zenkner works running at full capacity. The furnaces were always hot, and thick smoke emerged

After the Seven Years War, Empress Maria Theresia made »reparation funds« available to her subject Johann Leopold Riedel (painting by Wilhelm Camphausen, 1884)

from the chimney. Since the furnaces at that time were wood-fired, this works with its massive roof was located like all the others in close proximity to the forest. Extremely detailed agreements were negotiated with the forest-owning nobility concerning the use of this fuel. Nevertheless, this did not prevent a considerable amount of theft. However, because the glassworks were located in remote places far from the outside world – especially in winter when they were inevitably cut off by the snow – keeping a check on this was almost impossible.

One can sense the secluded location of Johann Leopold Riedel's Northern Bohemian Zenkner works from a description written during the period when many glassworks were founded – »The Clearing of Groß-Rohosetz Morchenstern Forest« dated 1687. According to this old description, the »third area of forest in the high court of Morchenstern lies for the most part in the high mountains. Let it be especially noted that among the Reichenberger Gränitzen on Noldenfluss Creek in a place of the same name, everyone has found a small meadow, built a glassworks and is able to make use of the woods.« The record describes the Zenkner works as a picturesque wooden structure with a high, steep, shingle roof and a long ridge turret. The name Zenkner came from the first tenant who, leaving unpaid debts behind him, »had fled with wife and child«. The name Antoniwald, the settlement close to the works, did not emerge until 1700 – in honor of the lord of the manor Albrecht Maximilian II Anton Count Desfours. It was customary to name places on the Morchenstern estate after the lord of the manor.

As ideal as the location of the Zenkner works might have appeared to begin with, Riedel faced overflowing order books and soon started looking around for expansion possibilities. In 1761, he leased the neighboring Karlshütte from His Grace Desfours and in 1766 the glassworks at Neuwiese from his cousin Johann Kittel. With the help of his cousin and his brother Anton – who was always dependent on the stronger Johann Leopold and died leaving debts in 1780 at the age of 36 – he managed to organize and run these three glassworks very efficiently. Three years later, in 1769, he also acquired the works at Friedrichswald.

Seen from today's standpoint, what Johann Leopold Riedel achieved may sound relatively simple. However, we have to envisage that period as it was then, when roads were in such a miserable state that the price of grain doubled when transported a mere hundred kilometers. Just one bad-weather period could plummet the country into genuine distress. In 1770, Gablonz recorded 91 rainy and stormy days in the middle of summer, and grain and hay rotted in the fields. Early the following year, such icy snowstorms swept over the peasants' fields that the next harvest was also destroyed during germination.

Agriculture was a hard business in those days anyway. Fruit and pulses did not do well, the meadows were boggy and could hardly feed the livestock (it was only after 1800 that methods were developed for draining meadows), the mountain soil was stony, and only in valleys was it possible to grow some rye. Thus, tables offered a meager fare. The people could count themselves lucky if they had bread made of barley and oats the whole year round; once flour was used up in winter, there was only thick soup made from pearl barley or

Prussian grenadiers shoot up window panes, and aided by the »reparation funds« Johann Leopold Riedel replaces them with bigger ones (colored drawing from 1758)

The exotic was in then – pair of long cups with elaborately feathered birds of paradise painted in bright enamel colors and with blue prunts (1881)

worker had to work one hundred days for a hundredweight of grain to make bread. But there was hardly any harvest work anyway, since the fields yielded nothing due to the impact of nature. And because the flax harvest had been destroyed, the weavers had nothing to do either. The livestock, for which there was no more feed, had to be slaughtered. Famine spread. People subsisted on dry grass and ground tree bark in order to survive. In the winter of 1771, typhoid broke out. Normally, some 65 people died in and around Gablonz every year; in the two years of famine and epidemic, the figures reached almost a thousand. Noted in the death records after the names of 221 persons are the words »fame obit«, »starved to death«. People called the fever the »hot bite«. The sick person became disorientated, trembled and shook with cramps and died very quickly. Compassionate neighbors placed food for sick people outside their front doors and then hurried home, so as not to have to see the afflicted crawling on all fours to get a meager meal.

Famine caused havoc throughout Bohemia, killing 250,000 people in this region within two years. Empress Maria Theresia in Vienna tried to alleviate the distress, waiving part of the peasants' taxes and investing two million florins in Bohemia. Her son, Emperor Joseph II, had the military granaries opened and rice and corn seed brought to Bohemia. This provided a little relief, but it wasn't until the rich harvest in 1772 that an end to the suffering really took place. More than thirty years later, a new famine epidemic threatened the people in the Jizera Mountains, but now the cellars had stores of potatoes – and slowly but surely the transport routes had also got better.

peas. Boiled carrots were regarded as a »delicacy«. Meat came onto the table only four times a year anyway, on the feast days. When young lads went dancing, they brought dried broad beans for their sweethearts. These were considered a treat. Diseases of the nervous system struck the population of the Jizera mountains with notable frequency, and goiter reached almost epidemic proportions.

The weather disasters in 1770 and 1771 meant a

Johann Leopold Riedel – flush with self-confidence from his success despite the difficult times – had, after a few years at the Zenkner works, cause to quarrel with the estate's head huntsman Josef Meschayda about wood deliveries. He was not prepared to be pushed around by the head huntsman. Meschayda reported the glassmaker to the manor administration, whereupon the Count Desfours made it impossible for Riedel to continue working. He refused to extend the lease in its previous form for the Antoniwald Zenkner works and the Karlshütte, proposing to grant Riedel only extremely distant tree-felling areas. This was an absurd proposal since it would have made operating the works completely unprofitable.

Ordinarily, this juncture could have meant another major crisis for Johann Leopold. By now, however, he had learned how to deal with such problems. His behavior suggests that he had apparently seen the break with Desfours coming. In any event, negotiations were rapidly conducted with Count Christian Philipp von Clam und Gallas, from whom he had purchased additional wood beforehand. Subsequently, this nobleman even allowed him to build a completely new glassworks – Christiansthal – further up the mountains at an altitude of 812 meters.

The talks between Riedel and Clam und Gallas must have been quite interesting and sophisticated, as Johann Leopold Riedel was a very strong personality. That must have impressed Count Clam und Gallas; and this nobleman, in turn, was a man of extraordinary presence, whose tact and perception led him to treat the glassworks tenant as an equal. This is the only way to explain how Riedel managed to impose his wish to conclude the contracts for Christiansthal not as a vassal, but as a free man. With the kindly support of Clam und Gallas, the great Riedel pioneer Johann Leopold received a letter of release in special recognition of his person and achievements from Prince Franz Ulrich Kinsky on February 28, 1776. Thus, Riedel the Third was now the first proper businessman in the family and forever released from servitude under the house of Kamnitz. At this time, Empress Maria Theresia was still on the Austrian throne. A few years later, when Maria Theresia's son Joseph II, her co-regent and successor, ruled the country from 1780 to 1790 as a reformer, the founder of the Riedel company might have had it easier. In the course of Joseph's enlightened absolutism, bondage was abolished in 1782.

This letter of release from bondage was initiated many months before its formal date. Accordingly, the agreement with the count concerning the construction of Christiansthal was concluded six months beforehand, namely on June 1, 1775. Both sides were well aware that Riedel would soon be a free man anyway.

As a result, the glassworks master obtained a dominical property measuring 24 acres and 205 fathoms for clearing and erecting upon it a »complete glassworks«, together with residential buildings and outbuildings. At the same time, »pasture rights necessary for the dairy cattle needed«, the building of a one-chute flourmill, of a sawmill, and the construction of two workhouses were approved, and he was also »licensed« for baking and slaughtering. Riedel obtained all the wood for building the settlement free of charge, with the exception of what he needed to build the sawmill. Every detail, particularly the works rent, was set down meticulously in the contract. And it goes without saying that the beer and spirits question also had to be taken care of in this contract. Riedel now had to procure alcoholic beverages from the Reichenberg manor office. At any rate, he got beer there at a better price than elsewhere, and spirits cost per pint a little less than in the tavern at Reichenberg (today Liberec). The buildings belonged to Riedel; but the lord of the manor, in whose hands the property remained, reserved an option for purchasing them.

The third Riedel, ever the dynamic entrepreneur type, hurried construction along – and was able to move into his new works by late autumn of 1775. The furnace was lit for the first time at Epiphany in 1776, and on Wednesday, January 17th, the first Christiansthal glass emerged. Five days later, the glass register, or sales list, was started. On January 25, the glass merchant and customer Johann Vatter had collected an order from the new works by two couriers, which shows how quickly a multitude of products was manufactured: »60 mugs with handle; 24 3-cup sets; 9 4-cup sets; 21 6-cup sets; 24 butter bowls with stippling; 30 broth cups; 24 glasses; 20 glasses; 36 bowls; 24 lids«. The biggest demand was for cups of all kinds in all sizes and shapes, with descriptions like »gewunden« or »stampig« and all-but-forgotten sobriquets like »abspreng«, »butten«, »johannes«, »masonic«, »spaniol«, »lünzel« and »schleiflünzel«. In the years to come, Christiansthal, off to an excellent start as a new enterprise, was to expand into beads, buttons, apothecary bottles, flagons, blue salt jars, ruby beads, lamps and countless glass stoppers.

The famous *annagrün* uranium color: Invented by Franz Xaver Anton Riedel. Here it was chosen for a lidded cup from 1881

In a later chronicle, the following was written about Riedel's extremely successful start at the new works:

The fresh vigor Riedel devoted to his new creation was clearly successful; Christiansthal prospered from brisk business, such that he had to look into enlarging his properties.

Indeed, when his brother Franz Anton died in 1780, Riedel again took over the Neuwiese works.

He also knew something of marketing and understood how to gear up business at the *Neuhütte* (or New Works) as it was originally called. In the first year, the customers, most of them from the immediate vicinity, were allowed to buy the products on account.

The successful and now more mature Riedel felt more and more like a patriarch, responsible for the people working for him, yet not in the sense of hard and fast rules and regulations as laid down in the official works ordinances. As the boss of an insular forest glassworks settlement, Riedel lived in his own separate world, with very individual ways of doing things. For all its meagreness, this also had a very special charm.

By Legal Agreement the Underling Becomes a »Freed Man«

As an independent glass manufacturer, Johann Leopold Riedel (3) was able to expand his business activities most substantially by building his new glassworks at Christiansthal – for those times a large and modern settlement. A project of such dimensions was not easy to accomplish since special approval was always needed from the nobility. However, Johann Leopold Riedel managed to obtain his letter of release from Christian Philipp Count von Clam und Gallas and thus to negotiate a contract as a free man with the prince on June 1, 1775, ensuring him all the rights required for building and operating the glassworks settlement. The count showed great decency towards the successful glassworks owner, but at the same time also revealed himself to be a crafty individual: Riedel stood surety for the signed contract personally with his entire property and all the works buildings.

In order to be released from servitude, an extensive written document was necessary. Here are excerpts from it:

Be it here variously proclaimed and known, especially to those required to know it: That today effective at the end of this year free and open negotiations were conducted and concluded between myself, Christian Philipp of the Holy Roman Empire Count von Clam und Gallas of the Palace Campo and Freyenthurn, fair chamberlain of Their Roman Imperial Royal Apostolic Majesties and Lord of Their Manors Friedland, Reichenberg, Grafenstein, Lämberg and Brodec etc. as their high authority and one – the honorable Johann Leopold Riedel, glassworks master, hereinafter to be a right free man released from the status of Bohemian-Kamnitz subservience; to wit: In the so-called Hinter-Friedrichswald Forests of the Reichenberg manor between the two streams called Kamnitz shall be designated and cleared by the manor and forestry office a piece of dominical forest of approximately 30 or 45 half-acres for the construction and establishment of a complete glassworks under the local name Christiansthal including adjacent living quarters, stalls, sheds, room for stacking wood and pasture for the keeping of necessary dairy cattle […] In return, Johann Leopold Riedel shall build and expand the structures necessary for the operation of his glassworks from their foundations to their completion and henceforth, as long as he remains the owner of these buildings, shall maintain them. Likewise shall he be obliged to purchase and transport at his own cost all materials, whatever their names, required for the operation of the glassworks […] Johann Riedel is punctually to remit in two semi-annual installments annual rent for the dominical land and glassworks to my manorial Reichenberg coffers beginning in 1778: Land and works rent 7 fr. 30 kr., flourmill and sawmill rent 15 score 5 fr. 50 kr., wheat fee 22

A carafe from the Jizera Mountains around 1800. In a flower wreath with a bow are the initials AR for Anton Riedel.

fr. 30 kr., for 2 outlying living cabins 22 1/2 fr. kr. each. For any dairy or beef cattle that he, the works master or the miller, may keep over the summer a rent of 30 kr. is to be paid, whereby grazing that may be disadvantageous for wood growth is expressly forbidden by the manor authority; goats, on the other hand are not permitted to graze in the forests, punishable with the loss of same [...] And insofar as a quantity of beer, brandy and salt is required by a glassworks, so shall the glassworks owner be obliged that he does not introduce any foreign beer, brandy or salt, punishable with double compensation, but instead that he shall procure all three substances from my Reichenberg offices and, in order that he may be compensated for the long transportation route, a keg of beer shall cost one guilder less than the Neuwiese price – or two less than that of Scholtessen, Seidel brandy shall be one crown cheaper than at that distiller's price, while a drum of salt shall be sold for the standard price of 7 fr. 40 kr., whereby no remains shall accumulate – that the beer kegs shall not rot but rather everything be properly returned to the brewery. However, so that the obligations which he has negotiated can be insured, so shall the same submit as a security all his property in general, and specifically the works and all the other buildings built on the above-mentioned manorial dominical land, such that for any interruption of the pledged payment they can rightfully be confiscated and also sold. [...]

For the decree and also the record that this

A crypt chapel for the dynastic Riedel family in the Northern Bohemian Jizeras

negotiation took place and was concluded in this form with mutual respect and of free will, two identical copies have been written and one given to each negotiating party.
Witnessed this day at Reichenberg, June 1, in the year of 1775

Wenzel Paul m.p. Manor Inspector
Joh. Anton Rücker m.p. Office Administrator

Johann Paul m.p. Account Clerk
Josef Elstner m.p. Granary Clerk
Christian Philipp Count Clam und Gallas m.p.

Johann Leopold Riedel m.p. Glass Master and Owner
Franz Anton Riedel m.p. Glass Master as Witness

The Scene Changes:
The Romantic Forest Setting Gives
Way to a Huge Industrial Boom

Spared from Marauding Prussians, Riedel the Third Donates a Chapel

In creating the Christiansthal glassworks, Johann Leopold Riedel (3) gave a signal to the Gablonz glass industry – a signal of progress. Yet hardly were the glassworks completed and production successfully started, when the third in the family dynasty was again threatened by a severe crisis. He had survived a world-wide trade recession and just recently an alteration to his lease making the continuation of the Zenkner glassworks impossible. And now there was new trouble.

The new danger was directly connected to the Bavarian War of Succession. At the beginning of September 1778, the Prussians, who had occupied Reichenberg, went marauding through the countryside and were about to set the Jizera glassworks on fire as a reprisal against the enemy marksmen they suspected hiding in the forests. In these uneasy times, Johann Leopold Riedel proved not only to be a businessman with a sense for profit, but also a man of character. Despite the danger his new glassworks Christiansthal put him in, he used the dwellings of his high-mountain settlement to shelter several troubled families from Prussian-occupied Reichenberg and further refugees from the surrounding area. Lasting for weeks, they lived in daily fear that the Prussian soldiers would appear from the forest, attack the works and slaughter and torch everything in their path like vandals. But fortunately Christiansthal remained untouched. As if by a miracle, mighty thunderstorms and extreme rainfall set in, lasting for days on end. The forests turned into a quagmire, so that the Prussians got bogged down, finally had enough and angrily retreated. After long weeks of worry, the glass operations could again be fully resumed.

The location of Christiansthal might be described as romantic, but the twelve workers, living with their families in three small houses around the works, led a hard life in these highlands, particularly during the long winter. Since self-sufficient agriculture was not possible up there in the woods, people were dependent on expensive deliveries from the valley below. Especially in winter they could count themselves lucky if these deliveries actually made it at all. The glassmakers could hardly make both ends meet, invariably owing the works master money that had been advanced to them. A classic patriarchal system, as it was often customary in those days, was the order of the day on the mountain. Johann Leopold Riedel was addressed as »Herr Father«, a greeting that incidentally was adhered to for many later Riedel generations.

»Herr Father« was a strict but fair employer. He was capable of motivating his glassmakers to work as one with him. Many of them stayed in Christiansthal for a long time. Day laborers constantly turned up and moved on after a short stay, but at least happy for a time to spend the nights next to the warm glass furnace. His permanent staff enabled Riedel to provide continuity in glass production – a rarity in those times of countless vagrant workers. Soon Christiansthal became known as a glassworks that manufactured outstanding prod-

A group photo of proud Riedel employees at the Polaun bead factory (around 1900)

ucts – and in a pleasant atmosphere. Alongside panes and vessels of nearly all shapes, beads, stoppers and bottles made of pressed glass were made. Traders liked buying in Christiansthal because with the products, which they would then take to be cut and engraved, they did a roaring trade.

But Johann Leopold Riedel did not forget the Prussian threat, even if times were now peaceful again. He wondered how he could thank the Lord and hit upon the idea of donating a small chapel, where he also paid the priest once it was completed: Father Anton Kreybich stayed from 1780 to 1784 and Father Franz Starrey from Laun presided until 1820.

Marriages took place between various members of the Starrey and Riedel families, and the relatives of the now aged Johann Leopold assisted him in his glassworks. With time, Christiansthal became known in the surrounding region as a kind of spiritual center, something which cannot be attributed to the chapel alone. Riedel himself loved his Christiansthal so very much that he even had a small forest cemetery laid out where he was later buried.

After a stroke paralyzed his left side, Johann

In the early days of glassmaking, wood was needed to keep furnaces burning and make potash which was later replaced by soda (forest workers in the Jizeras around 1900)

Leopold Riedel retired from active business in 1794. He was to live another six years. In a chronicle appearing over a hundred years later, his life's work was judged very positively:

»The Jizera Mountains glass industry had fallen into a dangerous crisis through the decline of the glassworks in the first half of the 18th century, because the old glass master families had not been able to adapt their operations to the changed conditions and thus gave up their inherited occupations. Riedel was able to avert the stagnation threatening the Gablonz glass industry just in time. He had already learned how to adapt glass production to market demands which had achieved a more and more decisive influence through the glass trade, and soon there was no lack of unfinished glassware available. Without neglecting common hollow glass, he changed his operation to semi-finished products for the enhancement industry, which had long cut itself off from the glassworks association and was readily employed by busy glass traders. Untiringly willing to try new things, he managed to supply enough useable colored glass for glass notions and smaller items of glass merchandise. His adaptability in various directions enabled the Gablonz industry gainfully to employ an increasing number of people, which led to its major economic significance [...] Johann Leopold Riedel personified the revamping of the old Jizera cottage glass manufacture to suit the purposes of the modern glass industry; without his accomplishments this development would have been inconceivable. He kept to tradition only in its external form and trappings. Christiansthal, his personal creation, was one of the last glassworks in the Jizeras built in solitude, cut off from the world with all the pioneering romanticism of the older settlements.«

A history that sounds like a school report card – top marks for Johann Leopold Riedel.

So what happened to the Zenkner glassworks that Johann Leopold had to give up due to disputes over wood with the woodsman and Count Desfours? After all, it had great symbolic value as the birthplace of Riedel's independent glass production in 1756. What is known is that for forty years after the intrigues, it was operated by several master glassmakers until 1814, when another Riedel, this time Anton Leopold the Fourth, Johann Leopold's son, returned there. Afterwards, Franz Xaver Anton – the fifth in the dynasty – was to take over the traditional Zenkner glassworks, and keep them till 1844. Subsequently, Josef Riedel Sr. took over the lease, although, as »Glass King of the Jizera Mountains«, he favored quite a different business direction, certainly not the operational form of a forest glassworks. In this family, that kind of change was to come up a lot, after all, family traditions form strong bonds.

Out in the Wilderness:
Insular Life in the Bohemian Forest

A typical glassworks with a massive roof, in the middle of the Northern Bohemian Jizera woods: Children and old people, smelters and assistants, quietly sitting around the warm, red and yellow glow of the glassworks furnace like a big family after work in winter, in a large room, which got colder and darker towards the walls; poachers, snares in hand, roaming unerringly through the dense forest; sweating glassmakers, faces sooty, with a mug of beer in the hand, standing together socialising in front of the works during a break: People living close to the lonely forest glassworks of Northern Bohemia found themselves on a secluded island cut off from the rest of the world.

Christiansthal, built high up on the mountain, was one of these glassworks that led a life of its own in isolation. This small, secluded settlement was welcomed by Count Clam und Gallas. The wood in this region had no great value because the forests lay much too far away for the transportation available in those days.

This meant that the glassworks, with its large demand for fuel to keep the furnaces in continuous operation, could at least make good use of the wood, the glass master generally paying the forest owner a lump sum for the rights to it. As a result, many of the nobility leased their less accessible woodlands to the glass masters who petitioned them – which led to an increasing number of these glassworks being built in the Bohemian mountains.

Once approval for a works had been granted, glass production could be commenced – under mostly primitive conditions. On the whole, unfinished or »blank« glass was manufactured. After the cooling process, it was wrapped in straw for protection and transported to cutting shops for further processing.

However, wood was needed not only for heating the furnaces. It was just as necessary for obtaining the potash that was indispensable for producing glass – and not too little of it either. Potash is potassium carbonate, a white, crystalline, slightly water soluble potassium salt of carbonic acid, a basic raw material for glass production. Adding potash in glass production essentially breaks up the quartz grains and reduces the melting temperature. In the old glassworks, this was important because it was difficult to get the furnaces up to very high temperatures. The potash was made by mixing normal ashes in big pots with water, then letting the mixture simmer.

Glass is made up of various base materials that are fused so that the molten »mixture« does not crystallize when cooled, but hardens amorphously, i.e. becomes vitrified, brittle and translucent. In terms of physics, glass is an undercooled liquid, which becomes increasingly tough when cooling into a solid form. In the cooling phases, glass at certain temperatures assumes the viscosity in which it can be worked into solid shapes, for instance by a glassmaker through blowing and rolling.

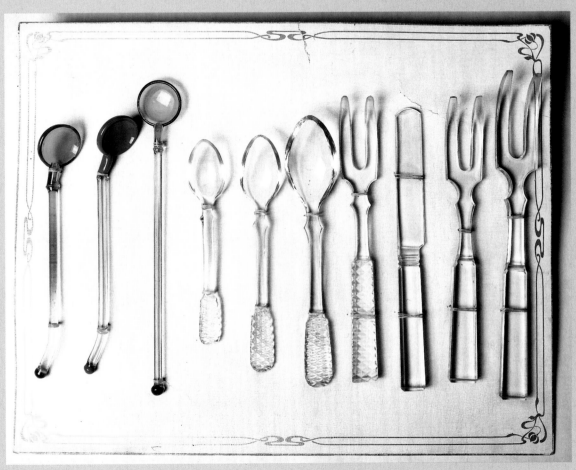

Sample card with glass dining utensils, produced by Josef Riedel, Polaun. The little clear and colored glass spoons were blown before a lamp (after 1900)

Glass basically comprises a mixture of silicic acid and metal oxides. Even in those days, a basic mixture was mostly – aside from additives that served special effects – composed of erinaceous quartz (sand), Glauber's salt, soda or potash, and lime or chalk.

This mixture was melted down with shards of glass, or cullet, in order to obtain that non-crystallizing, transparent material – glass. In those days, it was not all that easy getting that essential quartz sand either. You couldn't just order it like you can today. Usually, white pebbles were collected, heated as hot as possible, cooled down in water and then immediately chopped up and crushed.

At that time, potassium carbonate could only be obtained from potash. With glass production in-

creasing, it was foreseeable even in the era of the forest glassworks that the essential wood – the basic material for potash production – could get scarce: For the production of one kilogram of potash, one thousand kilograms of wood were needed.

True, mostly only low-quality brush and rotten wood were used. But it still meant stripping the forests. Particularly, when trees did get more frequently felled once the forest had been cleared of underbrush. A former forest where a glassworks stood could often no longer be called that after a few years.

Wood for potash was burnt on the spot, so that the ash needed only to be carried to the glassworks in sacks. Once the forest around a glassworks had been fully stripped, the works was often closed down. Without anyone to look after it, it finally turned into a ruin.

This must have happened pretty frequently, for in those days folks had a saying about these nomad people: »They burn the fence to sell the ash.« When awareness for the ravaged forests at last emerged, authorities attempted again and again to strictly prohibit the glass masters from removing wood from the forests – regardless of the threat to the glassworkers' livelihood. Only as potash was eventually replaced by the more expensive soda did the over-exploitation of the forests decline. It was not unusual for the conversion to soda to have been forced after the nobility began to restrict felling rights in order to protect the forests.

There was not much variety in the lives of people in the Bohemian forest works. The next village was at least an hour's walk away. There was only contact with the forester, who represented the authorities, and the priest, who took care of the soul. The forester, priest and glass master liked to play cards together, the fourth in the game being the village merchant or store owner, from whom groceries were purchased. But the glass master only came to the village every few weeks to cover his needs. These visits were like feast days, a welcome break from daily work at the furnace.

The estate administration was usually located even farther away than the village, and they had to go there to purchase basic materials for glass production, such as arsenic, white lead ore, chalk, saltpeter or salt. The estate administration was often near a town where oil, iron and paper could be had. For a glassmaker, his world ended here. What happened beyond that he only knew from hearsay. Often he did not really care either.

He did not have to set out for Spain or Russia to sell his glassware. More important to him was his glassworks, where the furnaces had to be kept burning day and night, and the forest that not only provided wood, but also mushrooms, berries, seasoning and medicinal herbs. He could use the water of his streams to drive the cutting shop and stamp mill. Fish and tasty crayfish lived in many of them – and if they were broad and deep enough, then the wood could be transported on them without any trouble.

Moreover, the forest provided very good meat. Many glassmakers were also game poachers, catching rabbits with snares or even shooting deer with shotguns. At the same time, the deep, dark forest with its hidden glades gave birth to count-

A selection of parasol handles from 1880 to 1920, partly painted

less tales of fairies, fauns and forest virgins, told on the long evenings among the works inhabitants.

In these glassworks, time had somehow come to a standstill. The products manufactured there were for a world which had nothing to do with that of the glass masters and his workers. In the forest, they lived as they had done for centuries, untouched by modern developments. The hierarchies were clearly defined: The master had the say, and the assistants had to come to terms with the fact that not everyone would become a master.

Assistants were needed *en masse,* since glass production consisted of a chain of different production stages. They were required in the glassworks, in the cutting shop, with the engravers, for glass fusing, as well as in the »pot room«, where the clay pots were produced, a kind of vat with a spout in which the glass was fused. Women, too, were known to work in the individual production stages. They cleaned the glass and wrapped it in straw. Even children did their bit by carrying the still hot glass to the kiln for annealing or cooling.

57

Particularly sought-after objects in distant India: Bangles, bracelets of colored glass – cut, painted and gilded (around 1920)

Glass workers were a tightly-knit community. Even the rogues amongst them, who moved restlessly from works to works for »traveling money«, were treated hospitably as a matter of principle. Young lads looked for girls to marry only in glassmaker families – no wonder that soon everyone was related to everyone else at some remove.

Knowledge of the art of glassmaking was passed down from family to family. They were proud of the tradition. The son did what his father had learned, no matter whether he was an assistant, cutter, engraver or gilder. Experience was thus never lost, leading to successive stages on the route to perfection in the glassmaking process. In some Northern Bohemian glass worker families, special know-how about glass fusing was treated as a professional secret.

Naturally, the nobility attempted to keep the glassmakers under control. In 1775, the lord of the manor, Franz Anton Count Desfours, imposed a series of new laws to this end »for all glass cutters of the Morchenstern manor, with which they must comply and also obey most precisely«. It stipulates: »If a stranger wishes to learn glass cutting, he shall be subjected to a 4 week probation, after which probation the master is free to treat him as he will.«

However, Desfours also intended with his regulations to give the underprivileged an opportunity: »If a poor man wishes to learn cutting and is unable to produce the funds necessary to be taken in, then his master will allow him to work this off against advances.« Although the local lord was responsible for beer distribution, he nevertheless was worried about the morals of the young people: »No apprentice shall enter a tavern nor shall he seek marriage without his master's prior knowledge and permission, and in case of violation he must stay in apprenticeship another day for each day missed.«

For the glassmakers, beer went part and parcel with their existence, raising their *joie de vivre* considerably. The glassworks principally procured the beer from the breweries of their lords of the manor because it was contractually dictated. In some cases, however, it is also recorded that the tenant received the right to brew the »cheap and thirst-quenching beverage for his people in their heavy work«. Fetching the beer from the glass master's wife or daughter was a task popular with the apprentices, since the beer was not precisely measured. And before the drink reached the workers, many a sip landed in the apprentice's belly. Beer was drunk daily in copious quantities – not only after the work was done, but also during breaks.

Here one must bear in mind that the furnaces never stood still and work went on long after midnight. If a furnace had to be replaced, which was very strenuous task, the master stood a keg of beer that was joyfully emptied. Beer was also the beverage served on the few festive occasions in the year, at the fair, on birthdays and at weddings. And although the people possessed very little money in those days, they nonetheless always came well dressed to these celebrations. Tailors traveled throughout the land, calling on the glassworks, not only to offer their services to the women, but also to take the men's measurements for their black suits – mostly by eye. Great care was paid to etiquette, unwritten rules being exactly observed

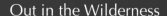

as a cultural value of the community. All festivities, even funerals, were very important for the people working in the glass trade. They were celebrated substantially and always as a large family.

In many instances, the glass masters got on very well with their workers, and they liked sitting together after work. If, however, the works master was a man from a better family who had been awarded the glassworks lease through nepotism, then the convivial get-togethers could prove a little more difficult.

Closeness was also made more complicated when some glassworks, like the Riedels', became ever larger and increasingly important. The glass master could no longer run everything by himself and now needed delegating skills. If the master had always been a patriarch for his workers, one who did not need written laws for dealing with his apprentices and journeymen, then his role became even more fundamental with expansion. He constantly had to consider how he was going to maintain control of the growing number of workers.

In larger facilities, the glass master would finally employ a works master as subordinate boss. Directly beneath him was the mold maker since he was able to read, which could not always be said of his masters. In the early days of glass manufacturing, the mold maker would chisel molds out of wood by hand. Later there were special machines that were driven by foot, enabling the desired molds to be lathed faster and more precisely. And because he was literate, the mold maker also had the job of telling the master – and also the works master – the order lists, so that they knew the number and fashion in which this or that glass piece was to be manufactured.

In the major glassworks, an important function was also held by the – usually better-dressed – cashier, a man with good schooling who rarely came from a traditional glassmaking family. When the works master yet again referred to the glass set »Klopatria« but meant »Cleopatra«, when »Sterling« turned into »Sperling«, and »blame« into »claim«, it was the cashier who offered a little tutoring, as reports from the time tell us.

Perhaps the cashier could not always be completely trusted, since he was the confidant and authorized signatory of the glass master, the patriarch; on the other hand, he was needed when an urgent letter had to be written with his assistance. At times, it was difficult enough not being able to read or write. For example, when a beer was ordered at a tavern, a notch was cut in two equally sized thin boards. Once a board was full and the day of reckoning due, the cashier or the similarly schooled mold maker would have to step in to work out the costs of the beer. After payment, the notches were simply planed off.

However, the cashier was important first and foremost as the person who paid the wages, board and lodging and any advances. And advances were frequently needed – for all celebrations and for the *Freispruch,* the »discharge« from apprenticeship to become a qualified master craftsman. Advances were also needed for basic things, like when a couple of pigs were to be bought for one's own use. If a worker accrued too much debt, then he would make off on the sly, leaving everything behind. Barring one thing: His toolkit. It was

The logo stood for quality: Silver company stamp with the form of a glass blower and the initials JRP
(Josef Riedel Polaun) on a cup vase in brilliant yellow (around 1930)

sacred to a glassmaker, and he never parted with it. A glassmaker without his iron – that would have been like a policeman without his sword. Incidentally, a well-skilled worker would also receive an advance when he moved to another glassworks. If he had debts, this advance was a purchasing price that squared, as it were, the debt with the old works.

Another important staff member in the larger glassworks was responsible for the administration of production, particularly for the proper packing of glassware in straw – some horse carts carried their

loads as far as Constantinople – and storing the glassware until it was collected.

The center of a glassworks was the furnace with the fuser or melter, his assistant and two stokers, called *Schürer*. An old works had many dark corners, but in the middle the covered light of the kiln glowed warmly. Here the glass was produced, and it was here that the conversion process from the coarsest to the finest material occurred, fascinating anew even the most hardened of glassmakers. Here, too, potatoes were roasted, and in the warm tunnel of the old furnaces, the en-

61

trance to the heating area, the day laborers and the sick slept, and children soaked from snowball battles dried themselves. When the furnace burned, radiated and hummed, it reassured the people, because its glow represented life and a future.

Often old glassmakers came by on a short visit, many of them suffering from cataract. Usually, they had no next of kin and were dependent on a hand-out, a hot meal. But they were popular guests because, traveling around so much they were invariably able to tell the latest news and gossip. So everyone would sit around the glowing fire-pit – beneath the service hatch where the pots were put in and turned, listening to exciting tales of adventure. For a glassmaker, this hatch was the very center of his life. Anyone who considered himself a true worker said he was born in the fire-pit.

What is interesting in the forest glassworks of those times is the role played by gold ducats. For individuals, gold ducats meant riches, but in the secluded glassworks, they were also used for making the color ruby-gold in the glass. This only worked with pure gold, of which the Italian or the old, yellow Austrian ducats were made; the later crown pieces could no longer be used for ruby glass, due to their composition.

The ducats were dissolved in a bottle of acid next to the warm furnace. This produced the tiny pieces of gold that settled at the base of the furnace pot when fusing. Gold ruby, or »the transparent red color« as it was called then, was first made successfully in 1612 by the Hamburg apothecary Dr. Andreas Cassius. A special acid was required to dissolve the gold into a very fine gold powder so it could be added to the glass melt. This acid was often also called *aqua regia* or »royal water«. It usually consisted of oxidizing saltpeter and non-oxidizing nitric acid, a mixture that was caustic enough to dissolve gold. (This, by the way, did not work with silver.)

One recipe called for a mixture of one part saltpeter and three parts nitric acid, while another required »17 drams of saltpeter for four ducats of gold«, the same amount of nitric acid and also a tin solution that in turn consisted of »a 3/4 dram of tin, 20 drams of saltpeter and 4 drams of nitric acid«. One old report even called for fusing gold ruby out of »ducats, shards, crystal, molten glass, antimonoxide and tin salt«. All these records show that there was a lot of experimentation going on. The lightness or darkness of the ruby glass depended on whether one used more or less gold.

Even the gilders, ornamenting the rims of the noble glasses with their creative painting work, used to work with gold paint produced from dissolved ducats. Thus, gold ducats were constantly needed in glassworks as material for work. But the temptation for some was simply too great, and it often happened that, despite all the precautions taken by the works owner, gold ducats or parts of them disappeared.

Modern techniques from the industrial age – such as gas furnaces or steam-driven cutting shops – brought many changes to the lives of glassmakers. In the summer, when there was too little water in the river, work in the cutting shop was simply suspended, and irregular fusing also meant work was only done as required. New technical achievements were to ensure regular, permanent opera-

tion. However, in contrast to other industries in which workers quickly turned into mere cogs in a gigantic machine, the work of the glassmaker retained a decisive amount of craftsmanship. The upshot was that glassmakers were able to maintain their way of life long after the days of forest glassworks had passed, right up to the First World War.

Anton Leopold's Problems:
The Napoleonic Wars Cripple the Glass Trade

In 1800, Johann Leopold Riedel (3) was laid to rest at the age of 74. After him, the Riedel glassmaking dynasty split into two lines that over time came to have no further close connection. The one line was known for glassmakers who energetically continued the tradition of art and production as it had gone on before. The other line also worked in glass, but its enthusiasm was somewhat dampened. It produced no spectacular developments like those in the main branch of the family.

After his father's death, Johann Leopold's second son, Carl Josef, took over the works in Christiansthal (today Kristianov), founding the second family branch that was able to navigate in calmer waters. He conducted his business steadily enough and was able to live comfortably. Up to 1945 this branch of the family was still active in the Northern Bohemian glass industry, and, in fact, it frequently shared common ground – even in business – with the main branch.

In terms of the dynastic development of an ever-expanding glass enterprise, the main branch of the family was continued by Anton Leopold (4), eldest son of Johann Leopold Riedel. Unlike his brother, Anton Leopold was very industrious, and from the beginning he was interested in not only continuing, but also optimizing the Riedel glass business. So, with much verve, he first took over his father's work at the glassworks in Neuwiese (today Nova Luka), paying particular attention to high quality and intensive customer care. He looked for new markets and was ahead of his competitors in introducing colored rod glass necessary for the production of buttons and beads in the growing pressed glass industry. (In the press works, buttons, beads and chandelier pieces were cut off reheated rods with special shears and pliers.) His instinct for marketability was incredible: So many orders came in that he was able to pass on some to his brother in Christiansthal. In business matters the branches of the Riedel family stayed in contact, but privately that contact faded.

The prosperous times that followed the death of father Johann Leopold (3) did not last long, however. Once again, commerce (in glass) was overshadowed by political decisions, or more specifically: By the Napoleonic Wars. These military conflicts crippled international trade; sales stagnated as a result, while food prices rocketed sky high – and the Austrian Bankruptcy Patent of 1811 brought a drastic currency depreciation. As if that were not enough, Polish marauders took advantage of the unstable situation to plunder the Bohemian countryside. All the glassworks suffered a major recession. Where once the iron rule was obeyed that the fires in the works were never allowed to go out, the emergency situation in many places forced them to be extinguished – sometimes for a year or more. A chronicle published in 1900 describes those times with typical pathos: »The fact is that the fluctuations in an unsteady world market cause tremors in the soup bowls of working class families.«

Anton Leopold tried new ways of getting out of his slump. At one point he took on the glass dealer

Before Napoleon reached Russia, his troops destroyed Bohemian houses that afterwards needed new window panes (painting by Vassily Vereshchagin, 1812)

Josef Pfeiffer as a partner. However he »couldn't stand the heat« and resigned because he did not believe the situation would improve. In fact, the Napoleonic Wars also painfully choked exports to newly independent America. The demand for mass-produced goods in particular fell drastically. One chronicler noted: »The French wars crippled foreign trade and threatened totally to put an end to the glass industry; great inflation and scarcity of money worried the workers.«

The recession left many resigned to their fate. The ever-optimistic Anton Leopold, on the other hand, counted on the wars to end soon and planned new activities. He spent long evenings thinking about the location of Neuwiese and came to the conclusion that it was not ideal for the demands of the future. A businessman in those times could not remain in the mountains of Bohemia. It was much too far away from the center of things to be able to react quickly enough during such crises to market opportunities and developments. The location in Neuwiese meant paralysis. Yes, Anton Leopold Riedel had honored and respected the legacy of his father, but now it had become necessary to leave the glassworks behind. It was not a betrayal of his father because he surely would have not acted any differently.

So, in 1814, Anton Leopold once again subcontracted the old, less out-of-the-way Zenkner works – and five years later he shut down production in Neuwiese for good. Now he was once again tenant, not owner, of a glassworks, but he felt closer to the more and more important industrialization process.

Neuwiese crumbled in the following years and in 1839 was pulled down. The one-time home of the Riedels was turned into a hunting lodge – and is still standing today.

Anton Leopold Riedel (1761–1821)

Anton Leopold remained restless, as if he sensed that he would not have much time for his task of shedding the era of forest glassworks and modernizing the technology of glass production. (He lived to be just 61). The dynamic businessman experimented with various production methods and looked for new forms of distribution. In addition to his industrial interests, he also had an eye for cultural values and founded a glass enhancement business in Meistersdorf (today Mistrovice) run by his two sons. However, that enterprise was given up after five years – decoration costs were too high, and debts had become too large. But as it turned out, one son, Franz Xaver Anton, demonstrated extraordinarily artistic engraving skill. He was a gifted glass artist.

This very fact made it worthwhile for Anton Leopold to run his enhancement business at a loss for a few years, for he had ambitions of emphasizing more the artistic side of the glass business. When he petitioned the Prague authorities for permission to describe his glassworks as an enterprise run »by Imperial and Royal Privilege «, he justified it with the special skills of his sons: »As it appears, my eldest son is so far advanced at glass engraving that his work has received the highest praise from his Majesty (!); my youngest son Josef has learned glass painting, so that on the strength of my products I can develop factory production for the general good.« Riedel accompanied that with an assessment by Trade Inspector Schreyer who was in charge of this region. In it Schreyer praises glass engraver Franz Riedel as »exceptionally gifted« and refers to the intensive export trade the company is doing in decorated glasses shipped to places as far away as Turkey, Naples and Russia. After the – in retrospect – incomprehensible refusal of this application, Riedel tried again the next year. This time it was supported by the regional author-ity of Bunzlau (today Boleslaviec), which especially praised the level of workmanship in the fine glasses designed by Franz Riedel.

Obstacles were being put in the way of the Riedels and their intention to gain more importance, despite their artistically valuable glass creations; apparently they were not to get that boost in image that would have come through the title of a glass factory with Imperial-Royal privilege. The title would have been important for the Riedels, not least because it would have meant the enhancement enterprise would have been a success.

In the family history of the Riedels, Anton Leopold (4) will not go down as the great man of action. His world was not one of spectacular change. On the other hand, with his calm and steady hand and unflagging optimism he led the company through extremely recessive times and was able to pass it on intact to his son. That was certainly no easy task.

When Anton Leopold (4) died in 1821, his successor, his son Franz Xaver Anton (5), faced rosier times. The economy was picking up, and the currently reigning *Biedermeier* style with its romantically idealized watercolors suited the Bohemian glassmakers well. They were heading toward a new boom.

Am I an Artist or a Businessman?
Franz Xaver Anton's Metamorphoses

Business thinking is often alien to gifted artists, particularly when it seems to be just about the dull facts of making money. How can you run a successful business and still maintain a sensitivity for the more delicate and subtle aspects of life? Almost impossible – but not entirely. Franz Xaver Anton Riedel, the fifth member of the family dynasty, was both a highly skilled artist and a talented businessman.

It was his artistic side where Franz Xaver Anton's personality first began to develop. As admired and praised as he was for his engraving work, this was not enough for him. Franz Xaver Anton carried something else within him, a head for business, which was in fact a typical characteristic, a specific gene of the Riedel stock. He wanted to set something in motion, produce like his ancestors and be a force in the universe of glassmaking. And so, after his father's death, he took over the tenancy at the glassworks in Antoniwald (today Antoninov).

In the era of Franz Xaver Anton Riedel, just as his father had predicted, the economic situation continued to improve. Economic paralysis lay in the past, and – this time in a big way – a new epoch of worldwide demand for Northern Bohemian glassware began. Gablonz (today Jablonec) notions (smaller items of glass merchandise) like buttons, beads and small bottles were now in huge demand – in America as much as in Africa. Here the export-orientation typical for the Riedel Company again became apparent. The Riedel glassmakers have been globally active entrepreneurs from the very beginning, always with a sensitiveness for markets in distant lands; and North America has to this day been a major source of sales. In good times this has meant a lot of success, occasionally even huge profits. Moments of economic crisis, on the other hand, have brought great problems that had to be prepared for in advance during prosperous years like those Franz Xaver Anton (5) enjoyed.

This boom under Franz Xaver Anton was connected to the first actual mass industrial production of glassware. Anton Leopold (4) had laid the framework for it. In the second half of the 19th century, Franz Xaver Anton's successor, the »Glass King« Josef Riedel (6), was to bring this success to its

Franz Xaver
Anton Riedel
(1786–1844)

greatest height and establish Riedel as the leading glass company in Northern Bohemia and all of Europe. Franz Xaver Anton's activities as the fifth of the Riedel dynasty can be seen as a kind of link between the old era of forest glassworks and modern industrial production.

Franz Xaver Anton Riedel was indeed a businessman but still remained an artist. He marched to two different beats. The works of art that he designed became more and more refined. Today various museums exhibit cups beautifully engraved by him, and visitors admire their craftsmanship. The specialized magazine *Weltkunst* extolled the virtues of his talents in a 1993 article entitled »Franz Riedel – glass engraver and industrialist in Bohemia«. It presents in detail various glasses created by Riedel, and the author, Sabine Baumgärtner, comes to the following conclusion:

All the stylistic features described here create a fairly complex picture of this glass engraver's *oeuvre*. This lets one surmise that his work is not only significantly more extensive but also, more importantly, far more variable than has been assumed up to now.

She writes of his designs for glass objects:

Characteristic for Riedel's work are various decorative elements, prototypical of the tastes of the time, that he gives a very distinctive, almost unmistakable, expression, making it possible, even within a certain room for variation, due to the form of the design to identify it as his and to ascribe it to Riedel with some assurance.

The author also recalls the years in which Franz Xaver Anton Riedel's father ran a glass enhancement business just for his sons, so that Franz in particular could live out his artistic side (see previous chapter):

The eye-catching craftsmanship of his son was surely one of the reasons for the Neuwiese glassmaker Anton Riedel to set up an enhancement business.

Of course, Anton Leopold Riedel had other reasons as well. His presence in the glass industry could not be dominant enough. After all, there were serious competitors, not many, but some. For example, there was the Southern Bohemian Buquoy glassworks, which was successful in fine glassware, as well as the nearby Neuwelt glassworks in Harrachsdorf (today Harrachov). Also, because of the customs frontiers Napoleon had set up, a broad company portfolio was certainly an advantage. This was why he gave his son this opportunity, even if the yields from the enhancement enterprise left much to be desired.

Franz Xaver Anton ran his enhancement business from 1809 to 1814 in Meistersdorf near Haida (today Mistrovice near Novy Bor), the most well-known Northern Bohemian center for glass decoration, but it only flourished in the beginning. The unfinished blank glasses, of course, came from the father, from the works at Neuwiese (today Nova Luka) and were then contracted out for enhancement by Franz Xaver Anton to nearby glass engravers and cutters. Even then, Franz was contributing his artistically best works. Particularly for individual orders of special objects he took up his tools and demonstrated over and over his highly developed artistic vein. And even if he was not »Imperially and Royally privileged«, his glass enhancement business was producing valuable works of art: A wealthy assortment of high-quality hollow glass objects, including engraved and cut glass drinking vessels, sugar bowls, dessert plates, bowls and mugs.

In their own way, the Riedels showed those stubborn Prague authorities who had dismissed their petitions for recognition in the area of glass enhancement what they could do: The new company in Haida produced such artfully designed glasses, bowls, vases, sugar bowls and plates in exceptional forms and of the finest workmanship that all the respected glass dealers throughout the empire soon became regular buyers.

Unfortunately, this business only held up a few years because it brought little profit, and even that disappeared when a new recession caused prices to shoot up. Franz Xaver Anton then had a lot of debts with his raw material supplier, who luckily was his own father. After five years, the family gave up this loss-making branch of the business.

But back to the mass products that sparked the big boom in the Northern Bohemian glass industry. The production of notions was soon running at full capacity, and the old forest glassworks now truly were a thing of the past. A decades-long era began which saw the founding of smaller glassworks for pressing, cutting and bead blowing. In the Kamenice valley a cottage industry emerged in which hundreds of families in the same area as the Antoniwald Zenkner works would purchase raw materials from the glassworks to turn

Riedel glass is distinct for taking great pleasure in experimenting with beautiful results: A vase out of black glass with wire mesh casing (around 1890)

them into mass fashion articles. For the founders of these cottage industries some two hundred years ago, this meant an endless amount of work for minimal wages. Their work was also dangerous to health. The lungs of glass cutters suffered from the dust; for bead blowers, sucking silver solution was a poisonous affair, and blowing on the hot flames was not exactly safe either. Many of these home workers died before they reached forty, and yet people still offered to do this kind of work.

It is hard to believe, but the worldwide demand for these colorful products actually rose and rose. In 1828, Franz Xaver Anton Riedel built an additional works in Klein-Iser (today Jizerka). On the outside, the nostalgic old style was kept, with the familiar low basement walls and the typical steep roof, but inside it was the very first of the Iser mountain glassworks with two smelting furnaces. While the works were still under construction, Franz Xaver Anton had a road built between Klein-Iser and Antoniwald on which he and his successors could easily travel back and forth between the works.

In the new Wilhelmshöhe works, however, enhanced cut and polished glassware was also produced – this particular Riedel would never be able to turn his back on glass of high artistic quality completely. Franz Riedel knew that his decorative style was very individual and hardly to be matched in aesthetic quality and perfection. Some of his very valuable work, which has survived to this day can be identified by the year and his signature. Particularly notable was the way this artistically ambitious Riedel graced trees and bushes with spheroid, feathery leaves. In the article discussed above, written in 1993, Sabine Baumgärtner writes:

Classicist vases, particularly monumental Louis XVI-style urns on pillars or plinths are among the objects he particularly favored. Along with symbols of luck and friendship, these are to be found on countless dedication glasses. Initials of names or monograms were mostly framed by larger medallions with decorative dewdrop borders and edging, another typical decorative element. One distinctive feature, however, has gone unnoticed up to now: The richly embellished trimming below the lip that is sometimes repeated around the base. Especially striking, for example, are the highly burnished dewdrop strings intertwined with leafy vines. Together with rosebuds or erect »pinhead« blossoms on fine dewdrop chains, they give the concluding rim above or below a special gravity. For some glasses, Riedel was satisfied decorating rims with a simple feathered vine frieze. More frequent, however, are the geometrical spheroid or ovoid cut bands. Conspicuous is the way the glass engraver constantly recombined the relatively small number of his prototypical borders and edging on individual glasses.

Franz Xaver Anton's primary business, however, was glass as a raw material, though here, too, he constantly developed new production techniques. In Europe the trend once again was forever more elaborate art glasses where painters, gilders, engravers and etchers outdid each other in their creativity. But the fifth Riedel followed this wave more as a hobby. He was, after all, a businessman and knew where money was really to be made.

Success confirmed that he was right. Better glass quality and interesting new colors like yellow and green uranium glass put him firmly on the cutting edge of the glass industry. Franz Xaver Anton named the two uranium colors *Annagrün* (or »Anna green«) and *Annagelb* (or »Anna yellow«) after his daughter Anna Maria (1819–1855). These exclusive names soon entered German as the common terms for what in English received the less charming name »vaseline glass«.

Like his father, Franz Xaver Anton was known for always keeping a cool head for business and stood for thoughtful and responsible company policies. The business was very stable, but he had no male successor. Now, this was a real problem for a dynasty where ownership had always been passed on to a suitable male heir without difficulty. From his first marriage, he had only his beloved daughter Anna Maria – and bequeathing a business to a woman would have been more than unusual in that patriarchal world.

In 1830, when he was 44, Franz Riedel brought his 14-year-old nephew Josef into the business. Did he know that with this choice he would not only save the Riedel dynasty, but that he had also brought a young man on board who, as the sixth in the Riedel dynasty, would overshadow all Riedels before him with his business acumen? One wonders. That speculation aside: Josef was the son of the glass painter Josef Riedel who, together with his brother Franz, had run the financially unsuccessful glass enhancement business established by the father Anton Leopold. After giving up that failed enterprise, the brother had changed busi-

Anna Maria
Riedel
(1819–1855)

nesses and become a merchant in Haindorf (today Hajnice).

Franz Xaver Anton quickly recognized that the younger Josef was a suitable successor. As a businessmen, he also did well to arrange the succession in time because Franz Xaver Anton only lived to be 58. After his death in 1844, Josef had to take over full responsibility at the age of 28.

In the 14 years with his uncle, Josef, an alert young man, had learned everything he needed to know about glass production. His first proper job at the works was as a clerk. »Clerk Pepi« he was nicknamed by the workers. They called him this with a touch of disrespect even though he was the owner's nephew. Pepi didn't care. Not because he had no character. On the contrary: The young man exactly knew his goal in his early years: He willingly took on any chore because he wanted to un-

A big hit around 1900, colorless glass vase with triple casing and an Asian-style landscape etched in

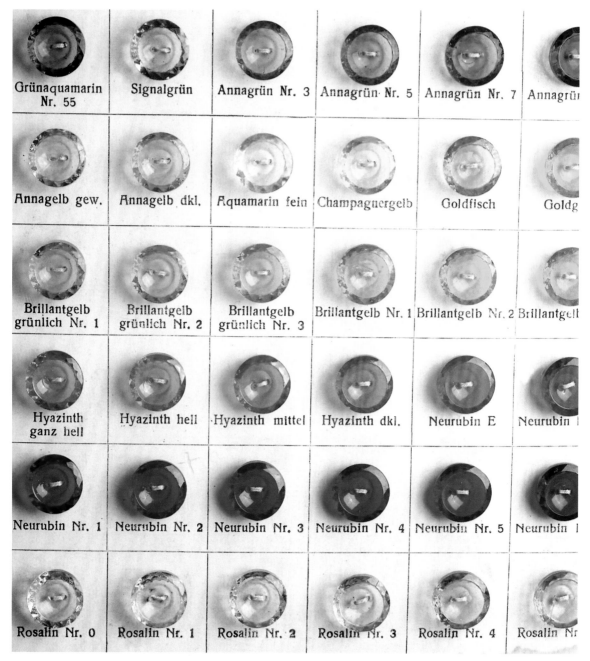

Grünaquamarin Nr. 55	Signalgrün	Annagrün Nr. 3	Annagrün Nr. 5	Annagrün Nr. 7	Annagrü
Annagelb gew.	Annagelb dkl.	Aquamarin fein	Champagnergelb	Goldfisch	Goldg
Brillantgelb grünlich Nr. 1	Brillantgelb grünlich Nr. 2	Brillantgelb grünlich Nr. 3	Brillantgelb Nr. 1	Brillantgelb Nr. 2	Brillantgelb
Hyazinth ganz hell	Hyazinth hell	Hyazinth mittel	Hyazinth dkl.	Neurubin E	Neurubin
Neurubin Nr. 1	Neurubin Nr. 2	Neurubin Nr. 3	Neurubin Nr. 4	Neurubin Nr. 5	Neurubin
Rosalin Nr. 0	Rosalin Nr. 1	Rosalin Nr. 2	Rosalin Nr. 3	Rosalin Nr. 4	Rosalin N

The finest nuances in color: On a sample card with glass buttons, for example, there are six different ruby glass tones and five shades of rosaline

derstand all the processes in the glassworks down to the last detail. And it came to pass that he quickly mastered every task. Soon there was no one who had the edge on him, and soon he was going to have the edge on other people. And not just the people at the glassworks. Josef Riedel (6), who was running the business shortly after his uncle's death, had big plans.

Bohemian Beads for Slave Traders:
Daily Life in the Land of the King of Glassmakers

What was work and daily life like for people in Northern Bohemia in the days of the Glass King? Today it is hard to imagine in any detail living through an economic miracle like the one in the late 19th century in which Josef Riedel's steady hand helped to lead the glass industry into the industrial age. Totally new production methods were gaining ground, lignite (or »brown coal«) was being brought in by train and cart, and railroad tracks were under construction, while at the same time the fathers and grandfathers of Northern Bohemia still told their children and grandchildren lots of stories about the old forest glassworks …

One of the most colorful and lively reports about this development appeared in 1876 in the magazine *Die Gartenlaube* as a large feature with the rather simple title »The Bohemian Glass Industry«. From various viewpoints, it recounts the years in which Josef Riedel helped to lead the glass industry in the entire region to its big breakthrough. Practically no other document shows so comprehensively and precisely what enormous importance the Northern Bohemian glass industry actually held for the late 19th century, how many families it fed but also how hard and unhealthy the work was (in which more than just a few children were also involved). It is a clever insight into the world of Northern Bohemia in those days that emerges from this report: Companies hardly play a role, and the name Josef Riedel, the King of the Glassmakers, appears only a few times.

No train passes yet from Reichenberg through the industry-rich valleys, something we rightly call incomprehensible, and we are forced, if we do not wish to go by foot, to make use of the post and stagecoaches which travel this way five or six times a day. The sojourner need not be concerned about his physical well-being, as there are sufficient inns everywhere. The delicious, golden beer is also never lacking anywhere or at any time, and it is with great satisfaction that the countless friends of superb drink will pay a – probably not short – visit to the Massersdorf brewery on the road not far from Reichenberg.

After a ride of an hour and a half, one arrives at Gablonz, a vibrantly prosperous, openly friendly city of seven thousand inhabitants. A few decades ago Gablonz was an unappealing, impoverished village and now the delivery junction for all the products is going up the valley for the flourishing glass industry.

Despite the low arability of the mountainous land that would not produce a tenth of the food the population needs, the less the area of four square miles that makes up the Gablonz and Tannwald districts had 50,000 residents, of them over 10,000 glass workers. In total, however, we find in this relatively small region approximately 30,000 people who earn their living from glass or its supporting industries. Only by these numbers, one recognizes that people here whether they are young and old, large and small, must give their utmost to receive wages which even then are often quite meager.

How different all of these occupations are, is demonstrated most clearly by a statistical table we acquired. According to this, the small region contains, aside from a number of larger works, 67 glass composition works, 250 glass press works, 400 cutting works, perhaps thousands of foot-driven wheels used to cut small objects such as beads and buttons, 160 glass lacing makers, around 100 bead blowers and 250 larger jewel smiths, these latter employing over a thousand workers.

However, one must not imagine any large factories among these glassworks and shops. On the contrary, the glass pressing works truly deserve their name (*Glasdruckhütte* literally meaning »glass press hut«), because in these wooden buildings completely blackened by smoke, there often is only room for one worker and his assistant. The production of glass notions is also almost exclusively a cottage industry. But we receive the best impression of the importance of the local work ethic when we are allowed to enter one of the large trading houses, which manage the sale of these products all over the earth. It is estimated that in the whole district there are some 180 glass export businesses, among which we find highly important companies [...]

Of great interest: In the illustrated family magazine *Die Gartenlaube* a report appeared about the life of Northern Bohemian glass laborers (cover from 1890)

The brighter the better: Beads and jewelry from Polaun reached ever farther into the African bush (lithograph from 1893)

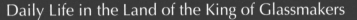

Glassmaking was once a man's world. With the rise of industrialization, the number of women in the Riedel bead factories grew

In addition to the numerous types of beads in all colors and sizes, it is also broaches, earrings, buttons, scarf pins, imitation jewels, crystal and the like that compose the full assortment which delights not only the savages of Africa and the transatlantic peoples, but also the European ladies and dandies. The markets for selling these sparkling objects truly span the entire world. The ledgers of the Bohemian companies speak of customers in all the larger ports on the five continents. To England and even France go masses of this inexpensive jewelry only to return to Germany, as imports, for three or four times their price. But the value of jewelry made of glass beads is likely to increase much more from when it is first made to its final sale. These are the necklaces, nose rings and earrings for African, Australian or South American ladies whose toilette otherwise requires but a square foot of simple cotton cloth while our European women and their manifold clothing needs call for measurements in square meters.

A full dozen colorful beaded necklaces here costs barely a guilder and particularly lavish specimens no more than two or three guilders. How gladly though does a hot-blooded black suitor on the Gold Coast offer the finest elephant tusk for such a bauble with which he can be sure to win the favor of his dark beloved! The big, bright glass beads are, in general, a sought-after article for the wild tribes of Africa who gladly trade the valuable produce of their land for them. It is well known that slave traders, with a string of beads purchased for barely a thaler, once easily acquired a negro on the African west coast for whom Americans gladly paid three hundred dollars.

To this day, such beads are being shipped in heaps to those lands where they serve as a medium of exchange and payment. We saw a shipment of no fewer than one hundred crates, which contained nothing more than strings of cherry-sized, ultramarine blue glass beads destined for Zanzibar as currency. The Sultan of Zanzibar, returning from a European tour, perhaps can fill the greatly depleted state coffers with this consignment. He certainly will not do bad business, for these beads, despite their pretty, shiny appearance, are laughably cheap. There are fifty of them strung on each string, and twenty-four of these strings, or 1,200 beads, cost no more than – twelve kreuzers.

The majority of the poor laborers who produce these beads in Bohemia are barely better off than the doleful slaves of sultry Africa. The thicker or thinner glass tubes, which we found being produced in the glassworks on our later wanderings, are turned into beads by workers who bring them to a vertically spinning, sharp metal disk which cuts off the individual beads. The pay for this work is so low that it is only calculated by the thousand-dozen, or twelve thousand, beads, for which the worker receives about twelve to fifteen kreuzers. The most industrious worker can only amass two thousand-dozen a day, earning him about thirty kreuzers (barely sixty pfennigs).

More lucrative, but also far more dangerous to health, is the making of beads blown over a lamp and then metal-coated. A white or colored glass bead is first melted at the lower end, and the glass is made molten again in the lamp flame then blown into very thin-walled balls. In front of our eyes, in an unbelievably short time, whole groups of these small and large balls are made, and a nitrate of silver solution is then used to give the necessary silver coating to them or the glass tubes which will later be turned into larger beads. The glass tubes or the balls are dipped into this liquid and, by suction with his mouth, a worker fills them to the top with the solution, holds the top

Great artistic skill: Drinking glass from 1820 with cut figure of the hunting goddess Diana. She is surrounded by Rococo ornaments and the initials FR (Franz Riedel)

end closed with his finger so that the liquid does not run out, and then pushes the bottom end into soft clay to close it. After the balls or tubes have stood for a time, the silver in the solution will have clung to their inside walls in a very thin but sufficient layer, and the remaining liquid is removed to be used again. The shiny gold balls and beads are made of yellow glass and also have only this silver lining. Many of our readers, however, would probably recognize these sparkling balls as the decorations on their Christmas trees, to the luster of which they contribute in no small way.

Humble Clerk Pepi Rises to Become the King of the Glass Trade in Northern Bohemia

The clever youth Josef had grown to become a sturdy figure of a man by the time of the early death of his uncle Franz Xaver Anton (5), and his bushy mustache was to become his trademark. Ten years after entering service for Franz and only four years before the death of his uncle, the Riedel succession problem was solved in an unusual way: After overcoming some family resistance, the 24-year-old Josef Riedel married his 21-year-old cousin Anna Maria, the beloved daughter of Franz Xaver Riedel. We no longer know whether it was Franz, naturally not oblivious to the intelligence, determination, business acumen and work ethic of his nephew, who carefully arranged this match, or whether it was just true love. An article from a historical journal in 1974 claims that when Josef asked his uncle Franz for Anna's hand in marriage, Franz accepted with joy. Within the year they married, the new husband and son-in-law Josef eagerly took the helm at the glassworks in Klein-Iser (today Jizerka).

The wedding came at the perfect time because Franz Riedel died four years later. His daughter was his sole heir. In this way, everything was perfectly prepared for the coming ascent of her husband Josef to become the glass magnate of the Jizera Mountains. This went in leaps and bounds, as Josef Riedel was apparently in a determined rush to capture the top position in the Northern Bohemian glass industry. He first ran the Wilhelmshöhe works (in Klein-Iser) which he then put in the hands of a relative so that he could bring the works in Antoni-wald (today Antoninov) up to speed. In 1849 he also bought a recently completed modern glassworks in Unter-Polaun (today Dolni Polubny). Changes came in 1848, the year of the revolution in which a constitutional monarchy was declared by imperial edict. Tannwald (today Tanvald) became an autonomous municipality and remained so until 1929.

A terrible private loss hit the quickly rising businessman in 1855: His beloved wife Anna, admired for her »kind heart«, died at the tender age of 36, leaving behind their sons Hugo, Wilhelm and Otto and daughter Marie. Nothing was going to keep Josef in Antoniwald any more, with all its memories of his deceased wife. In addition, the lease with Count Desfours had finally run out. To keep his mourning from weighing on him too much, Josef Riedel threw himself into his business. He concentrated especially on his works in Unter-Polaun.

The road through the mountains from Reichenberg to Trautenau (Liberec to Trutnov) which was commissioned by imperial edict on March 20, 1847, was nearing its completion in 1850; the roadway to Prussia was also being improved. Soon the Polaun glassworks was to enjoy an excellent transportation connection, and lignite, the current energy source of choice, could be brought in easily. On May 1, 1858, Josef Riedel relocated permanently to Unter-Polaun. Actually, it was not as attractive there in the narrow valley as it was on the enchanting 800-meter high Klein-Iser plateau, but the restless businessman preferred the proximity to

When Josef Riedel senior, »Glass King of the Jizeras«, died, he was accompanied by almost all his employees – a good 1,250 people

the wider world where he shipped all of his products. Josef Sr. built his lovely house in Unter-Polaun directly beneath the railroad viaduct so that he could always hear the rattling of the trains as the harbinger of modern times. A year later – fourteen years after the early death of Anna Maria – he married Johanna Neuwinger, a daughter of forester Neuwinger from Friedland (today Frydlant), chief forester for Count Clam and Gallas. At this time, Riedel owned the Wilhelmshöhe glassworks that he had inherited from his first wife and the works

in Unter-Polaun. In addition, he began the construction of another works in 1866 next to the one in Wilhelmshöhe to replace the traditional Antoniwald Zenkner works. Because business was going so well, another works was added in Wurzelsdorf (today Korenov) in 1867 where he, almost as an afterthought, also built a cotton mill. The Wurzelsdorf glassworks, however, was closed after fifteen years due to a lack of wood. Decades of strip logging had decimated the forests.

No one could stop the rise of Josef Riedel (6).

He not only sold his glass products in Germany, France and Italy, but was also active in distant countries in Asia, Africa and North America. Riedel was a classic entrepreneur: An excellent bargainer, a remarkable strategist, creative in his range of products and very socially conscious with respect to the well-being of his employees. But he did not only have a lot to do as a businessman. He was also honorary curator for Northern Bohemian industrialists, a member of their municipal representative board and of the chamber of commerce. He was particularly sought after by the committees of the chamber of commerce for his acumen and his self-assured judgment. He also took on tasks in the community, and, as if he did not have enough to do with his many businesses and honorary positions, he also worked as a member of 16 different associations.

Later, his four sons, Otto, Hugo, Wilhelm and Josef (from his second marriage), were to work at his side in the large-scale business. In this way, an additional glassworks was set up in Maxdorf (today Maxov) – and in 1880, when Josef Riedel was already 64 years old, another large glass factory was opened in Unter-Polaun. Having by then long been called the Glass King of the Jizera Mountains, he showed no signs of wearing with age; he refused to rest, and progress was his formula for eternal youth. After the Austro-Prussian War of 1866, the economy ran perfectly for a few years. In 1868, Riedel – whose far-sighted business policies absorbed the economic ups and downs – introduced gas furnaces, ending the strip logging of forests. The necessary coal came by rail, which, due to a concession in 1872, finally reached Tannwald in 1875, now arriving even more easily than by the

The Riedel villa in Polaun – it still stands today, but after the confiscation of 1945 it is no longer owned by the family

new mountain road. The train went from Eisenbrod (today Zelazny Brod) near Prague – which had a direct connection to Prague – through the Jizera Mountains via Reichenberg and Gablonz to the train station at Tannwald (which at that time had 2,400 inhabitants of mostly German ethnicity), with its romantic setting, and then finally on to Schumberg (today Zumberk). Coal modernized the manufacturing processes, helping the Glass King to guarantee the dependable continuity of the by now huge output of glass at his works.

Josef Riedel paid great attention to two areas of

his empire. With a knowledgeable hand for management, he guided the expansion of the company and the more and more complicated marketing of his range of products. At the same time, he worked tirelessly on the permanent modernization of his production facilities because each technological innovation streamlined and perfected the production of glass. His raw, prism, press, rod and cane glass was primarily marketed in Bohemia, while the articles from his bronze-ware factory, glass enhancement works and bead facilities mostly went abroad. One special technique of the Polaun Riedel works was the insertion of metal mesh in the outer surfaces of cylindrical cups, classes, bottles or jars.

The factories of Josef Riedel – five glassworks with a total of fourteen furnaces, a cotton mill, a loom, a bead factory, the enhancement works and the bronze-ware factory – were a driving force throughout the region for developments in both technology and society. His factories employed 1,300 people, and in the region several thousand more people worked for him, from cottage industries to distribution. They all participated in the life's work of one of the great industrialists of the Austria-Hungarian empire.

When work ended at the glassworks in Wurzelsdorf in 1872, Riedel had the building refitted into a workers dormitory for the nearby cotton mill. The Glass King made sure that his employees were well cared for, and he did not consider them beneath him, but rather as being at his level, and so with time they only referred to him as »Father«. Clerk Pepi had figured out in his early years how to motivate people.

Josef Riedel did not hide in his office, but instead, when innovations were on the cards, he took part in the chemical and technological experiments. He impressed his employees with his excellent knowledge of works furnaces. Although he had money, power and influence, his employees felt he had remained one of them. In 1870, he bought the natural spring in Wurzelsdorf for 6,050 guldens, complete with its little bathhouse. The place had been known for a hundred years as a healing spa called »Milchbrünnl«. In response to legends about the excellent effects of the spring waters on human health, the valuable water was examined by the University of Vienna. In fact, the »miracle water« was found to contain many healthy trace elements and minerals, and in 1849 the bathhouse was built with first three, and then seven pools. Glass King Riedel was excited about the remarkable healing effects of the waters of Wurzelsdorf and bought the spring.

Naturally, he also turned that into a profitable enterprise. He applied to the regional authority of Gablonz for a permit to build a new bathhouse – and got it in 1872. Then he completely refitted the old bathhouse and had a beautiful, path-lined park laid out around the spring. A lovely, small-scale spa area emerged. This business also flourished, though Riedel had not intended to make money out of it. The first people traveled to Wurzelsdorf for days, even weeks, to treat their various ills in the spring water. Feeling better after their stay, they spread the word, and more and more people in need came to experience the powers of the spring for themselves.

To give thanks for his great fortune, the Glass King also had the local parish church renovated, giving it a new organ, an altar and the most beautiful chandelier throughout Bohemia. As a rule, he was very socially committed, known for his numerous voluntary donations. When another recession set in between 1888 and 1890, his majesty, Emperor Franz Josef I gave the needy 6,000 guilders »with wholehearted intent«, Count Desfours donated 1,000 guilders, but Josef Riedel, without fuss or much ado, provided 10,000 guldens. It was little wonder that the Glass King was finally honored with the Knight's Cross of the Order of Emperor Franz Josef.

He had a constant eye for technological innovations. On July 17, 1883, the 63-year-old patented a »new method for the production of blank glass in round and angular tubes with small hollow tubes in their walls«. The patent for the internally ribbed tubes includes the following explanation:

> The glass which the glassmaker requires to make rod glass for beads is not produced in the usual way by gathering from a crucible and forming a parison, but rather a specially designed mold gives it the shape (façon) necessary for drawing the glass into hollow tubes.

Josef Riedel was just as committed to the magic of glass as a material. He never lost his personal passion for glass and its practically endless possibilities for the most wonderful metamorphoses. In 1886, he succeeded in melting glass in the Venetian style. These new products from Bohemia meant a huge boost in sales. A particular creative achievement recognized to this day was the use of uranium oxide for the legendary »Anna colors«.

It is difficult to gain a complete sense of the enormity of the Glass King's achievements, so the companies he founded are presented chronologically below. This list demonstrates Josef Riedel's wise method of tending to the important infrastructure of glass production and illustrates how active he remained far beyond the age of sixty.

1849: Purchase of first Polaun works
1866: Construction of second works in Klein-Iser
1867: Construction of glassworks in Wurzelsdorf
1875: Stake in railroad line Eisenbrod-Tannwald-Polaun
1878: Construction of glassworks in Maxdorf
1880: Construction of second works in Polaun
1883: Purchase of coalmine in Hundorf/Teplitz (today Hudkov/Teplice)
1883: Construction of bronze wares factory in Polaun
1883: Founding of glass enhancement factory
1885: Purchase of glass enhancer in Herrachsdorf
1886: Construction of third Polaun works (Przichowitz)
1889: Construction of fourth Polaun works (hollow glass works)

In 1891, three years before his death, the Glass King, by then 75 years old, introduced a new labor policy with benefits far ahead of their time. Employees now enjoyed greater social care, particularly a company medical plan which in case of illness paid daily compensation, treatment by a physician and medicines. The passage covering the medical plan stipulates under the heading »Caring for the sick and injured«:

> 7. For the sake of supporting sick or injured employees, a company medical scheme exists

into which every member including the company owner shall pay a regular fixed premium. The scheme guarantees free treatment by a doctor, free access to medicines, daily sick pay and a contribution for funeral costs. Further stipulations are to be found in the legally approved statutes of this scheme. All civil servants and workers with mandatory insurance are insured by the *Unfallversicherungsanstalt* (Accident Provident Institute) for Bohemia in Prague.

This policy also gave workers access to better education. The section »Schooling for minors working as assistants« states:

> Apprentices [...] as well as assistants up to the age of 18 are to receive the necessary time for visiting vocational evening and Sunday classes.

In addition to requirements for employees, the policy also provided a right for »justified complaints«. With regard to working hours, the company »Jos. Riedel Polaun« also reflected a move toward a more socially minded era. Now most workers were guaranteed to have Sundays and holidays off, and production was slowed down for these days:

> On holidays, as well as on the evenings before major public holidays, there will be a reduction of activities at factories; the appropriate time will also be granted for the requests of employees to attend holy mass. On Sundays and major holidays, being Easter, Pente-

Josef Riedel senior (1816–1894)

cost and Christmas, general work will cease, and only the heating of the glass furnaces and other necessary plant facilities and cleaning activities at company locations will be tended to [...] A worker employed more than 3 hours on a Sunday will receive the statutory respite as compensation.

Particularly interesting in the Glass King's labor policy was the section on job protection: »An employment relationship still exists, even at times when work is reduced or a plant has to be temporarily closed.«

These social achievements make the Glass King special. But that was not all. He became a more and more adept manager. No wonder that, in light of such convincing economic success, Josef Riedel Sr. became, so to speak, the undisputed ruler of the Jizera Mountains region. But for him it was never

Table adornment for the 40th anniversary of Josef Riedel junior's employment. Engraved is the motto: »True to ancestry, the eye on the future! 1882–1922«

about power. He remained fair and just, always thought of his employees and of the common good. The Glass King was an exceptional person who also happened to have the great good fortune that his activities took place during fairly peaceful and stable time in terms of politics. Relatives in neighboring towns could not compete with him. They themselves had their own respectable success as mid-sized glassmakers, but did not come anywhere near the main Riedel line with its enormous business achievements. Thus, even though family contacts had ebbed in the previous decades, the relationship remained friendly.

When the Glass King of the Jizera Mountains, the »Father«, died on April 24, 1894 in Polaun (today Polubny), he left his son Josef Jr. (7) with a glass empire without peer in the whole world. And he left a socially peaceful region, which he had constantly supported. At his funeral, his glassmakers carried him to the family crypt accompanied by hundreds of workers. 20,000 guilders for the construction of a poorhouse, 30,000 guilders for its operating costs, 7,000 guilders for the poor fund in the eight towns with Riedel plants, and also generous payments for his workers and relatives, for his servants and the Polaun charities: That was the last will and testament of this truly great man, who, with all his power, money and influence, never lost his love and appreciation for people.

In his day, Josef Riedel Sr. had risen to be one of the most important industrialists in the Austro-Hungarian Empire of the late 19th century. He was a pioneer of the modern industrial model. The special position and success of the Gablonz glass and jewelry industry are closely connected with him: Josef Riedel influenced the development of Jizera Mountain glassmaking from a small business to a major industry in the region that employed some 300,000 people by 1945. The second volume of *Die Glasindustrie* (»The Glass Industry«, Vienna 1898) describes the Glass King as follows:

The name Josef Riedel Sr. is inseparably attached to the flowering of Gablonz industry, and one can call Josef Riedel the motor for this industrial development. In the drive to adapt his products to the needs of further development, he established the bases for new products and knew how to equip his companies with all the latest technologies. After more than 60 years of work, he had brought his business to such a height that upon his passing (1894) it encompassed five glassworks, two glass enhancement plants, a plant for making *façon de Venise* beads, two textile looms, a cotton mill and a bronze-ware factory.

A »Grand Array of Brimming Beer Mugs« for the Glassworker

A job in the booming glass industry was tiring, but more important was that everyone had one. The second part of the detailed *Gartenlaube* report relates the situation of cottage workers and glassmakers:

On our wanderings in this heavily populated area, the peace and quiet in the towns of the cottage glass industry is conspicuous. On the highway one most commonly meets people delivering their products in small bundles to the trade houses for which they work.

Those returning carry material for more work at home purchased at blank glass plants with a part of their profits. Long lines of heavily laden carts carry stacks of large and small crates to the next railroad station, from which the goods begin their journey across the sea to the distant corners of the globe.

It is a hard life that the residents of the mountain villages lead. From their earliest years, poor children already have to help at home and contribute to the often meager wages. Little children, often only three or four years old, have to string the beads on threads which the father, mother or older siblings have pressed or cut, or they have to affix buttons or various types of jewelry to cards.

The slightly older children already have to use heavy shears to remove edges left on pressed glass in order to prepare it for cutting. It is often touching to watch these poor children attentively and enthusiastically do the work given to them.

Only fleetingly do they glance with yearning outside at the beautiful mountains or the bit of garden in front of their houses where only butterflies and beetles can play undisturbed. The hard-working children here play a game called work, and life presents them mostly with a future of endless struggle and toil.

What a bustle there is in these simple, but always well-kept homes, where the workroom as well as the kitchen must often enough serve a role as the living and sleeping quarters for the whole family! Two or three workers will sit with a boss at one little table. Each has the simplest kind of lamp in front of him: A small earthen vessel in which a wick fueled with bits of tallow burns. Some may even can afford the more expensive petroleum for their lamps.

Under the table, each worker has a bellows installed, which is kept in constant operation by foot to create a jet of flame through a pipe that leads upwards to the lamp. Through the addition of lead oxide a glass rod is easily melted, and the glass former brings it to the flame with one hand. With

Pretty vessels for women's scents: Ruby glass and dark blue-green copper glass perfume bottles (1840–1850)

his other hand, when making a button for example, he takes pincers to hold a metal prong upon which he applies the glowing glass, which is molten as sealing wax, until the button has achieved the prescribed form.

In this state, if it is to be decorated, selected metal foils or pieces of glass colored with other patterns are affixed, and then, before it is completely cooled, the finished button is pressed in a metal mold which also gives it a richer shine. Flowers and all manner of objects are fashioned in a similar free-hand way, showing us the worker's sense of form at its peak […]

The route to the Polaun glassworks near the main road passes through long rows of massive piles of lumber, from whose ashes, like the Phoenix, a more beautiful, shining entity will emerge. This glassworks currently produces only white crystal.

The white-hot molten mass roils to and fro in two gigantic pots. The formers and blowers lift small and large quantities of the searing liquid up out of the furnaces and blow it into delicate glasses or flagons or use molds to press it into substantial objects. Of course, all of these articles require laborious, careful polishing so that they may charm us in all their splendor.

As interesting as all the tasks in a large glass-works are for the viewer, for the workers themselves they are toilsome and wearing. The usual five to seven hours in front of the white-hot furnace, which we dare not ap-proach within more than a few steps, but also the glass blowing, which is so damag-ing to the lungs over time, are unfortunately well-suited to adversely affecting the lives of these people.

The mighty furnace: In this heat, raw materials are melted into liquid crystal glass. This requires temperatures of over 1,400 degrees Celsius

Riedel glassworks in Polaun: Many employees lived in dormitories built for them in the area

Some of these workers at the furnaces earn six guilders or more a day. But the larger part of this seemingly large wage is spent on food. The incredible thirst which a raging furnace causes resists water and can only be properly stilled with beer; at least that's what the workers claim.

But then, to overcome this fiery foe, such a giant array of brimming beer mugs is necessary that a ration of this size cannot be had for less than two guilders per day. Along with this, the heat and work bring about a gigantic appetite which, because the body must be strengthened, is not to be sated by potatoes and dry bread alone. Thus, one indeed may understand why only the lesser part of this seemingly large wage remains for the family [...]

Annually, the three Riedel works produce thirty to forty thousand hundredweights of glass for which they consume eight to ten thousand Austrian cords of wood. In the earlier wood facilities, approximately forty percent more wood was consumed.

However, when one considers the number of smaller glassworks and furnaces we encounter here, one must bear in mind with concern the ever worsening destruction of the forests, despite their fabled wealth of wood. The tripling of the price of wood means that this deforestation has no foreseeable end.

The best protection for these mighty forests will finally come with the eventual completion of the railroad line which has been projected for years from Reichenberg to Tannwald or on to the Silesian border. The

93

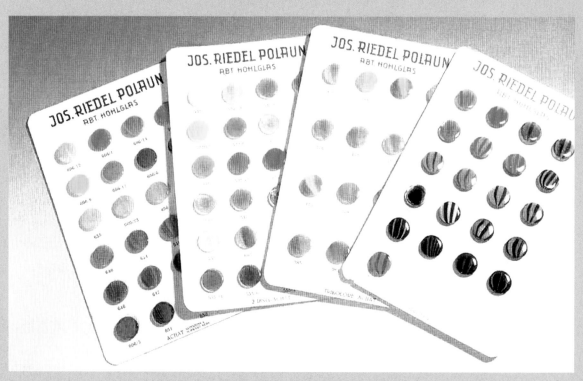

Picking a color is no easy task with this selection: Sample cards from the glass factory Josef Riedel, Polaun, with bright glass buttons

bustling industry in the area alone is more than reason enough for this improvement in transportation. But once cheaper coal can be brought in as a substitute fuel for the thousands of work fires, the mighty forests will be protected in due course and preserved for the general good of the region […]

In between the dark pines on the banks of the rushing Jizera River lies the village of Wurzelsdorf with its handful of houses, known in the area for some years for a spring with healing ferrous and sulfurous waters. Once a rickety wooden hut with a few very simple pools was all there was to find here.

Now there are several handsome, well-kept buildings, which offer the visitor the most hospitable of welcomes. The total refitting commissioned by Josef Riedel makes it self-evident that profit was not its primary motive, for the prices compare very well with the tariffs and taxes of other, even much smaller, spa villages […]

And so we bid farewell to these lovely, prosperous Bohemian valleys; rarely has an-

other region been able to offer so much of interest in such small an area. And we wish for the Bohemian glass industry that its products may spread the fame of German diligence to all corners of the globe for many, many years to come.

Deep Yellow, Carnelian and Coral Red: Josef's New Colors and his Love of Glass

Josef Riedel Jr. (7) was born on February 20, 1862. He was one of the tycoon's sons. And he was only 32 years old when Josef Riedel Sr., hailed as the ruler of the glass market, died in 1894. Perfect conditions for the son, in the seventh generation, to fail miserably.

But this Josef Riedel Jr. did not suffer under the weight of the life's work and gigantic achievements of his father, the Glass King of Northern Bohemia. He was no daydreamer, no failure and no gregarious idiot spending away his inheritance. All these potential negative developments in sons of powerful, dominant and extremely successful people are familiar; there are psychological studies about them, and books and films have studied this problem. In fact, it is not unusual that the scion of a major industrialist, an exceptional leader, finds no useful purpose in life but rather, at best, chooses to remain a son for a living. This observation may explain in part why track records of individuals often burn out like shooting stars and thus why old family dynasties like the Riedels are rare.

Generational conflicts and family discussions are only fruitful if the son of a powerful father is not defeatist, doesn't feel his »back is against a wall«. Only then can a future heir develop his own room for maneuvering. It is only in this way that the continuation of a family business is possible over the years.

Down through the generations, the various leading fathers in the Riedel family have apparently understood this well. To this day: In 2003, for example, Georg Riedel, the tenth in the dynasty, installed his 27-year-old son Maximilian as CEO in charge of the very important American business. And even back then, when the Glass King, Josef Riedel Sr., was pursuing his truly unique career, the son never let himself get discouraged. As in all Riedel generations, Josef (6), the father, gave his son the freedom to develop his own way of continuing the business. From the start, Josef Jr., a child from the Glass King's second marriage, did not try to copy his father's success in every field. He knew well that he would only become an admired and economically successful part of the family chronicle if he could achieve things in the glass business in other areas than those of his father, whose business pioneering set historic standards. But one thing was as present in him as it was in his father, the Glass King: A great love of glass. And yet, even then, the successor would only make it if he dared to engage in tough but constructive conflicts with his father, articulating his own ideas. Josef Jr. dared to, and in the end the powerful father appreciated that his son was a man of character.

The son of the Glass King quickly learned the ropes and demonstrated an astonishing feel for the processes involved in glass. He attended university in Dresden and the *École de Chemie* in Mühlhausen, Germany, at that time the most renowned school in the field. He had an interest in science and developed many new techniques that are

Extravagant form: Rectangular vase in ruby red painted in white enamel and gold leaf with bronze attachments

still applied to this day. For example, he oversaw the development of the so-called »flowing« colors. This technique enabled yellow to run into deep yellow and for blush pink to run into carnelian red. Under his leadership – he officially began employment at his father's company in 1884 – also the bronze-ware factory first began the application of molten metal on glass. He continued to research and experiment tirelessly and he set up the first glass laboratory in the Northern Bohemian glass sector. The many processes he patented included a machine for stringing beads. After ten years he finally succeeded in developing a machine that mechanized the drawing-out of rods and tubes necessary for the production of

beads from one to four millimeters. The development of this machine was a milestone of sorts because it greatly facilitated the processes involved. The fourteen- and fifteen-year-old *Springerjungen* (literally »jumper boys«, or runners) who were once necessary could now breathe easy. The drawing-out process used to require that these boys had to rush back and forth along the drawing corridors, which in the large works were up to 200 meters long. Each runner clocked a good 30 km per day. The new apparatus cut this task down to a few meters. This improvement in Rocailles bead manufacturing ensured that the works in Polaun would maintain a dominant position in the sector for decades.

A document from 1877 described the original way in which glass was drawn out:

First the »rods« are drawn out. A lump of glass weighing several pounds is wrapped around a gathering iron and worked. A waxed, compass-like tool is stuck into it as it is alternately rolled on an iron plate and dipped in water. A bit of the glass (called the »rose«) is gathered from it with a second iron. This bit is stuck in the hole of the larger lump (»gather«), and then a boy runs with this iron down the drawing corridor. All the while the glassmaker (»drawer«) sheds the soft glass from his iron, creating a long tube barely thicker than a needle. After the rods have been cut into pieces, they are sorted by thickness, and then the cutters take them and cut (or snap) them with shears.

This constant running along the drawing-out corridors was exhausting, making Riedel's new machine with its big wheels a sensation. He received an official patent for it in 1896, »a privilege for an apparatus for the drawing-out of molten glass into tubes and rods«, which almost completely relieved the drawer. The invention suited the thinking of Josef Riedel. In this way, he combined his delight in technology with an alert interest in people and their tasks.

Actually, with regard to the human aspects of the workplace, he was very much raised in the spirit of his father. Even the smallest possibility for improvement caught his interest. He was the first glass industrialist to pay thorough attention to the lung problems of glass workers, and in 1904 he

donated a lung treatment center to the municipal hospital in Tannwald. Together with Dr. Schwertassek, pupil of the famous surgeon Theodor Billroth, he sponsored studies that enabled the distinction between lung ailments as occupational hazards and other types such as tuberculosis. Before then, there had been no clear diagnosis criteria for distinguishing between silicosis and TB – tuberculosis had also been incorrectly diagnosed as a glass worker illness. As a result, living and working conditions were studied more closely, and various preventative measures against silicosis were introduced.

A document from 1895 describes glass work at the end of the 19th century as follows:

For the most part, glass is drawn into more massive rods or thinner canes and given in this form to glass pressers and flame workers; or hollow rods are made which bead blowers or cutters process further. The glassworks also produce thin-walled balls which are cut into smaller pieces with a diamond and polished and then given to glass assemblers [...] Smaller glassworks with one furnace in which the so-called »composition«, glass with high lead content, is fused in clay crucibles (usually six, also two, or even just one) so it can be drawn into tubes and rods, are called »composition burners« here. There are several of these as well in the district, in Gablonz, Albrechtsdorf and Joseftal. The thick, solid rods are for pressing, and the delicate tubes (hollow and solid) which are produced there in every imaginable color, are for flame workers. Besides the usual colors, practically

Inspired by a shell: Atlas glass bowl of light blue opal glass and increasingly dark pink casing (around 1885)

every composition burner has its own colors the others do not offer; the way these colors are fired, or made, is their secret and their art.

At the turn of the 20th century, the Gablonz region was a gigantic network in which thousands of people earned their daily bread through the multifaceted production, processing and working of glass. As a result, hundreds of thousands of colorful bracelets went to India, for example. From 1859 to 1869, the 164 km-long Suez canal was built and was a neutral shipping lane after 1888 (the canal did not come under English protection until 1936). For exporters, shortening the sea route to Asia by some 10,000 km meant an improvement that was like a dream come true.

Josef Riedel Jr. (7) was the market leader particularly in blank and pressed glass. He employed over 400 glassmakers and blank glass makers – and about 20,000 German home laborers from the frontier region around Gablonz worked with blank glass while another 6,000 people in the adjacent Czech villages blew, pressed and cut factory-purchased blank glass. The next group in the glass chain were the traders with their worldwide markets. The heavy industrial producers and the traders, in other words the first and last in the chain, made the big money. Their workers still earned decent wages, but for the home laborers things were tight; they were hard pressed by prices and competed with each other. Small strikes were launched from time to time, but guaranteed minimum prices still couldn't be pushed through. Because of the promise of social security and decent wages, however, there were no complaints from the Riedel employees. Riedel, by the way, even in these boom years, had remained in the background as what one might today call a »private label«. Aside from various products directly from Riedel, the company delivered the balance of its output to wholesalers and sold under other brand names. Riedel was known, but its degree of familiarity did not at all reflect the economic weight of the company in the glass sector. And despite the fact that nearly every Riedel generation produced its own achievements, that put the company far ahead of its competition in terms of creativity.

Josef Riedel Jr. shone with his extensive research and the technological innovations that resulted. His chemistry training was especially helpful when he transferred the science of colloids, which he had learned while studying under a colloid researcher, to the medium of glass. Colloids (suspensions of metal compounds) could be used to color water – and Josef Riedel succeeded in transferring this process to glass. Using compounds of ionic and molecular pigments (sulfur carbonate, cadmium sulfide) and colloid pigments (silver, gold), step by step various green, yellow, orange and ochre shades were developed for transparent and opaque glass fusings.

At the end of the 19th century, it was hard to keep up with the growth of technological innovations in the industry. As always, the opportunities these developments presented for streamlining processes endangered the older ways of working. And thus it was with bead making, too.

In 1886, Josef Riedel Jr. brought a new glass chopping machine from a trip to Venice that rendered the previous method of cutting off beads from rods one at a time by hand obsolete. With a kind of comb, the machine pulled through up to 50 sticks at a time in an even pace, while a guillotine-like steel blade clattered away at the rods in a steady, rhythmic up- and-down motion – and that 75 times a minute. The rods rested on lower blades that touched the glass in three places; these gave it an additional blow when the top blade hit. In this way, 60 kilograms of glass beads could be produced in ten hours. However, this achievement put the hand-cutters out of work, as their traditional manual labor only produced one kilogram of beads in fourteen hours.

Two years after the first glass chopping machine was imported, Riedel opened his own glass bead factory in 1888 – and set up 38 of these automatic cutters. Thus, in this business segment alone, he achieved a daily output of several tons of beads.

Yet, Josef Riedel Jr., did not only feel committed to technology, research and development but also to ethical values. After all, by the time he died, he employed more than 3,200 people. For that reason, he had worker apartments built according to the latest hygienic standards and was known, like all the Riedel generations before and after him, for his respectful treatment of his employees. His workers

As a material, glass offers lots of possibilities: Crystal and uranium glass *(annagelb)* desk set. Thermometer has a centigrade and Fahrenheit scale (before 1914)

honored and respected him, even when they at first had difficulty accepting some of the technological innovations and their streamlining effects.

In all his activities, Josef Riedel Jr. never collided with his two half-brothers from their father's first marriage to Anna who had died young. The brothers were also active in the glass business but without much inspiration.

Josef Riedel made different business decisions than those his father made. He was not interested in buying more and more plants. His main emphasis was not on expansion because he knew that the company already was sufficiently large. Additional acquisitions would – rightly – be seen as solely serving power interests, not any sensible growth.

Further expansion could ultimately lead to a collapse – today, managers would call it overkill. »Jos. Riedel Polaun« was supposed to be large and strong in a healthy way, not mutate into a decrepit dinosaur. The father had made the company large enough, now the issue was developing further strengths.

In 1906, an exhibition of the Gablonz glass industry was held in Reichenberg. An accompanying brochure for this important exhibition gives a sense of the role of the Northern Bohemian glassmakers in the era of Josef Riedel:

Above all, it is the glass and textile industries which have made German craftsmanship from Bohemia famous throughout the world. Over the centuries in which they developed, these two outstanding local German specialties have earned international repute. The history of German Bohemian glass can look back on a proud past, and nothing in the world has become as popular as German Bohemian glass. Its history stretches way back to the Middle Ages. The wealth of lumber in the heavily forested frontier mountains of the region provided the most natural conditions for establishing glassworks [...] And if informed voices today declare that the German Bohemian glass industry is the highlight of every world exposition, then one must consider that proud past which first led to the domination and fame of German Bohemian glass throughout the world [...] The collective exhibition of the »Glass Industry of the Jizera Mountains« (products and blank glass from the company Jos. Riedel, Polaun, and the articles made from blank glass by their customers) – 54 exhibitors – is intended to represent the whole glass industry of the Jizera Mountains with their own objects made from the company's blanks [...]

Among the colors used, the coral red which had been a dream of glassmakers for centuries deserves special notice. Two years ago, the company was finally able to fire this long-sought red and thus fill the spectrum of colors with every imaginable shade between orange, crimson and purple. Luxury objects show the same feature combined with black and green Empire-style flashing and decorated with solid bits of ore-tinted glass. Ruby red has the same importance for transparent colors that coral red has for the opaques. Its deep reds remind of the most vibrant copper rubies but are far more translucent.

Glasses produced for technical uses also enjoyed praise. Riedel received first prize in Frankfurt for its bobeches, crystalline saucers at the base of candles on chandeliers. Josef Riedel also invented a groundbreaking waterproof streetlamp that is also described in the brochure:

Among the products from the enhancement works are the waterproof streetlamps and fittings on display in which all the metal parts have been completely imbedded in glass, a better insulator than porcelain, hard rubber etc., completely avoiding screw holes. The glass protective cap and the bubble surrounding the bulb are cut to match each other and protect the inside of the lamp from caustic fumes, moisture and dust. They have proven themselves well in outdoor installations, in damp spaces and for underwater uses.

The passage about the amounts of glass produced gives another impression of the importance of the Riedel glass company at the time of Josef Riedel Jr.:

Josef Riedel junior (1862–1924)

Contributed to by 54 exhibitors and organized by the company Josef Riedel, Polaun, the exhibition also offers a comprehensive impression of the countless products and blank glasses made by this international firm as well as the many objects its customers create from the blanks. Having joined the glassmakers of our sylvan mountains in 1752, the house of Riedel has conquered large parts of the region, now supplying in the truest sense of the word the main part of the glass which is to be further worked [...] According to M. von Tayenthal, at the beginning of the century the Riedel Company in Polaun, with its seven glassworks in Polaun, Wilhelmshöhe, Przichowitz, Neudorf and Maxdorf, produced 21 metric tons of hollow glass, 20 t of solid rods, 92 t of bottles, 1,699.3 t of pressed glass, 1,157.2 t of hollow rods and 815.4 t of cane, a total of 3,804.9 tons of glass, of which, according to the same expert, around 3,000 tons were passed on for further working. Calculating into that expert's estimate that the other glass companies together produce, for further working, 40 rods, 25 canes, and 20 bottles and articles of pressed glass for every 100 from Riedel, one arrives at a figure for the total annual amount of glass being worked in the Gablonz industrial region of around 4 million kilograms.

By itself, the company »Jos. Riedel Polaun« produced 2.8 million kilograms of glass for further working, and another 700,000 kg came from the other branches of the family also active in the glass business. That meant: Seven eighths of the glass being worked in Gablonz was produced under the Riedel name. In other words, the brochure from

1906 shows how loudly the glass industry's motor in Northern Bohemia roared, at the kind of high and healthy pitch that many businessmen today so fiercely crave.

This splendid glass exhibition famed throughout Europe was followed by another revival in the market sparked by the impressive results of the first glasses colored with selenium and cadmium. Josef Riedel Jr. had developed them using his profound knowledge of chemistry. He had no way of knowing in 1904 that his technique of bringing out colors perfectly in glass – especially the complicated red – would cause another jump in sales with the invention of traffic lights two decades later.

When the seventh Riedel developed his selenium ruby for glassmaking, colored glass was still only mostly used for aesthetic purposes or occasionally for pharmaceutical containers. But even then, it was already being used for the production of early forms of »cat's eyes« whose enormous relevance for reflectors in the later automotive boom could not have been anticipated. The son, Walter Riedel (8) – similarly technically and chemically inclined – would later play a major role in that development.

Selenium-colored ruby glass resulted not only from Josef Riedel's creativity but also from his general passion for enriching the variety of colors: It was he who, due to his brilliant chemical knowledge, was to expand the spectrum in glass production to an unbelievable 600 colors. The extensive technical knowledge necessary for such an unmatched multitude of hues and the brilliant utilization of the fantastic possibilities for bringing glass to its fullest beauty with exquisite colors is no long-

The opening of the Suez Canal on November 17, 1869 meant big business: It was finally easier to ship wares to India (contemporary watercolor by Edouard Riou)

er to be found in most glass companies today. Josef Jr. also drew his remarkable innovative strength from the cultivation of the best people in his glassmaking company. This made it possible for him constantly to achieve the highest levels of quality for his products.

For example – following in his father's footsteps – he helped his glassmakers buy land and build homes. In this way, he strengthened the glassmakers' connections with the company.

He also furthered employee care through a works physician, the medical plan and the pension plan that the Glass King had introduced decades before it was legislated. This was the only way to assure the company would be run by the next generation with commitment and responsibility. In this respect, Josef Riedel Jr. was thinking in dynastic terms.

At least he could assume that his son Walter, born in 1895, would one day lead the company in the right way. From early years, he had the impression that Walter's seriousness and technical talents would at a later date bring the skills necessary for assuming control of the business empire.

Josef Riedel (7) was thoroughly satisfied with his work and life. His plants saw one technical innovation after another, his glass objects were becoming more refined every day and the succession seemed assured.

However, World War I put an abrupt end to the good times – at least for the next few years to come. Walter, his son, was in Italy as a soldier and the world market underwent fundamental changes. Countries where huge volumes had once been exported, particularly overseas, were suddenly striving for more independence – resulting in the loss of a lot of business. The Riedel Company was once again painfully feeling its dependence on exports.

Right after the war, the situation was no better. An ardent admirer of his emperor, Josef Riedel was disturbed by the fall of the Austro-Hungarian monarchy. Bohemia was now part of the new Czechoslovakia. How would that affect the future?

One of the last measures Josef Riedel Jr. intensively pursued before his death on January 30, 1924, was the comprehensive preparation of his sons Arno and Walter for the task of leading the company, particularly its expanding activities in technical glass and other specialty glass for the Gablonz economy. In these years, Josef Riedel's nephews Otto and Waldemar were also involved until, by agreement of the family council, his son Walter (8) took over the company.

After the passing of Josef Jr., the company was in a difficult situation: It now had five co-owners. There was Wilhelm, son of the Glass King from his first marriage with Anna and by now 75 years old (who died in 1929), as well as the grandsons Otto (1881–1934) and Waldemar (1886–1959). From the Glass King's second marriage there also were the grandsons (the sons of Josef Jr.) Walter and Arno Riedel.

But even then, one thing was clear for the family: If the company were to split apart while being passed on from one generation to the next, the dynasty's thread that had been so strong up to now would come unraveled. That was prevented with a clear decision to install the highly talented Walter as company director and executive officer, though

Walter and Arno received equal financial shares of the inheritance. It also came to pass that the family branch from Josef's first marriage eventually died out.

In his last will and testament, Josef Riedel Jr., who died at the age of 61, bestowed the poor with the considerable sum of 150,000 guilders – much in the tradition of his father, the Glass King.

Red – Yellow – Green: The Traffic Lights

The Riedels and their business enterprises had always had a green light. »Stop« or standstill were simply no options for this family.

However, road traffic in the cities of the Industrial Revolution was constantly threatened with standstill – far into the late 19th century. There were more and more cars but still no proper traffic ordinances. New York, Berlin, London, Paris were already metropolitan giants with urban centers. Here, life on the main streets was fast and furious, it was noisy, and more often than not, intersections were endlessly jammed.

For safety reasons, policemen were stationed at the most chaotic points to bring some order to the horse carts, coaches and automobiles. They had little effect. Thus, in 1868, a monumental, towering structure was erected in London, a predecessor of the traffic light. It consisted of a lamp holder that could be turned with a lever and had integrated red and green gas lights for »stop« and »caution«. This ingenious innovation, however, suffered a bitter blow to its image on January 2, 1869, after only a few months in service, when it blew up with a huge bang and seriously injured the policeman on duty.

In the decades that followed, the Riedel glass company benefited from the development of technical glasses that could be colored and used in signal lights on ships or lighthouses. The Riedels had always been leaders in colored glass. Their spectrum of colors was almost as extensive as all the conceivable shapes glass could take. Now with the new pigmentation process using selenium and cadmium, glass could be offered for industrial uses in deep red, green and yellow – and, most importantly, in perfectly even shades. Rear reflectors for cars – no problem for Riedel; colored plates for electric traffic lights – basically no effort at all. The only difficulty was that no one had yet invented it.

Finally, one was put up, not in New York, not in London, but in Detroit. After all, the assembly line production of the legendary Ford Model T had made the United States the most motorized country in the world at the beginning of the 20th century – and Detroit was, after all, the home of that car company.

The inventor of this colorful set of flashing lights was a policeman named William Potts. Day after day he stood in the busy intersections of Detroit, watching helplessly as honking cars and their cursing drivers maneuvered their way into snarl-ups from four directions. No wonder he had the occasional passing thought that things could not go on like this. But what could help? In this state of urban desperation, he thought of the electric signals on the railroad. Then he came to the simple conclusion that such an apparatus ought to work for street intersections, too.

It did. However, it took a little more tinkering because on the railroad it only regulated a linear, parallel traffic situation. The situation at an intersection with all kinds of vehicles coming from different directions was, without doubt, a bit more complex. After chewing it over a lot, Potts finally had the inspiration: Where the railroad needed two signal lights with two different colors to keep trains from colliding, a street intersection would

Colored Riedel glass regulates heavy traffic: Traffic tower with clock in the middle of Berlin's Potzdamer Platz also houses traffic light with red-yellow-green glass (around 1930)

need a three-colored model to avoid crashes and endless jams. Best would be red, yellow and green, then a couple of electric parts to coordinate light switching, and *voila!* On January 2, 1919, fifty years to the day after the explosion of the gas monstrosity had decimated traffic light enthusiasm, the new traffic lights began operation on one of the wildest corners in Detroit. A year later, the motor city already boasted fifteen of these

devices, and in New York, too, more and more intersections were tamed using the new electric light system. The uncontrolled anarchy of car drivers was at an end as people waited, more or less patiently, through the red phase before starting up again with green – a feature of civilization that has ruled to this very day.

Despite Potts' grandiose invention, European attitudes towards it were more skeptical. The first

PUSH
BUTTON
WAIT
YOUR
TURN

STOP

110   Pedestrian light with manual operation in America. The first functioning traffic lightwas invented in Detroit

German traffic lights were not installed until 1924 at Potsdamer Platz in Berlin. Its lights were lined up horizontally until two years later an improved, vertical model from the Siemens Company replaced it. In Milan and Rome the first traffic lights came into use in 1925, and in London the urban domestication of the motorist with the red-yellow-green color method began in 1926 at Piccadilly Circus.

Mr. William Potts was unfortunate as – like many inventors before and after him – he forgot to patent his ingenious gizmo. That was first done in the United States by Garrett Morgan in 1923. Out of respect for Morgan, one must say he did not just borrow other peoples' ideas. He constructed the first fully automatic lights, meaning a policeman no longer needed to stand, watch and switch the lights by hand.

Now, however, saucer-sized, clear glasses in perfect red, green and yellow (later amber) tones were required. This was the shining hour of the Riedel Company because it had developed and mastered the difficult technique of brightly coloring and processing glass. That also gave them the know-how they later needed for the production of headlight glasses.

amarin
55

Signalgrün

Annagrün Nr. 3 | Annagrün Nr. 5 | Annagrün Nr. 7 | Annagrün Nr. 9

gelb gew.

Annagelb dkl.

Aquamarin fein | Champagnergelb

Goldfisch

Goldgelb

Brillantgelb
ünlich Nr. 1

Brillantgelb
grünlich Nr. 2

Brillantgelb
grünlich Nr. 3

Brillantgelb Nr. 1 | Brillantgelb Nr. 2 | Brillantgelb

Hyazinth hell | Hyazinth mittel | Hyazinth dkl.

Neurubin E

Neurub

Brilliant Technical Achievements under the Pressure of War

Arming, Disarming, Retooling:
Turbulent Times between the Wars

If a man is a genius in his profession, it can bring him satisfaction, success and money. If he is a good person as well, then this can also be his undoing. Walter Riedel (8) was such a man – and he went through heaven and hell.

The life story of Walter Riedel shows like no other in the Riedel dynasty that ups and downs in life follow an apparently unavoidable law. But it also shows that a person at his lowest point, with a certain self-confidence, ruggedness and a trace of optimism, can survive even the darkest moments. Walter Riedel was one of Europe's biggest industrialists for years, but then, after the end of World War II, he had to endure expropriation and internment for ten years in Russia.

Before the start of the First World War, Walter Riedel studied at the University of Technology in Dresden, Germany. With an extensive education, especially in technical issues, he returned to the family villa in Polaun. It quickly turned out that he had inherited a lot from his ancestors, and in an almost perfect mix: From his father the characteristic of basing his thinking on clear scientific principles and from his grandfather, the famous Glass King, a head for business and a bold corporate vision; from his other grandfather – a classical officer in the Habsburg military – he had inherited a willingness to act. And from all the Riedels he inherited an openness for the needs of his employees.

In World War I, the son of Josef Riedel was ordered into Italy as an artilleryman and mountaineer. He performed his duty selflessly and returned to Polaun with decorations. Walter had already begun to work in his father's company during the tough postwar period, and shortly after Josef Riedel died in 1924, he took the helm. As outlined previously, this happened by consent of the family council, following the proven Riedel maxim that keeping the family business intact for a successful future meant keeping it in one set of hands. Any overly complex partition could mean the death of the long-lived dynasty. No matter whether it was business concerns, research and development or technological innovations – Walter Riedel showed he was competent in all areas. And also self-confident, particularly with regard to his father's intellectual legacy: After Josef's death, Walter Riedel quickly changed the company logo. Yet another clear sign that from one generation to the next there were always conflicts, or at least very different views.

As co-owner of the company »Jos. Riedel Polaun«, the eighth Riedel brought about the first collective contract in the glass industry, the wording of which was still an industry standard fifty years later. In the following years, he was to reorganize most parts of the business in a way that greatly streamlined processes but did require employees to take large cutbacks. »Jos. Riedel Polaun« remained an extremely productive enterprise with an excellent social climate.

His decisions may in retrospect appear to have been a matter of course, but far from just growing up to be rich, the heir of a dynasty also has to take on a huge responsibility. It is his express duty to preserve and further develop the company – as in the case of the Riedel glassworks. The livelihoods of many families depended upon it.

The first big test for Walter Riedel was the global economic crisis in the late 1920s. The crash of the New York Stock Exchange in October 1929 soon also sucked Germany into its maelstrom. National protectionism spread. From 1929 to 1933, Germany's exports shrank from 13.5 to 5.7 billion reichsmarks, and unemployed figures rose from 1.3 to 6 million. Walter Riedel did what he could and ran things hoping to keep damage to a minimum by remaining flexible and adopting measures unusual for a glassmaker. First, he jettisoned the unprofitable cotton plants (the protectionist Czechoslovak national policies had already helped to turn the previously prosperous textile sector into a lossmaker), but in the former loom in Wurzelsdorf he set up a factory for artificial sausage skins, which was soon very profitable. It was Walter Riedel who was first to find a practical solution for the production of collagen casings. A remarkable achievement for an entrepreneur who was a newcomer to the field.

On the outside, Walter Riedel looked nothing like a tough man of action. He was very straightforward, but also a friendly, polite and patient man known for his seriousness at work. But those who knew him, were well aware that no obstacle deterred him. On the contrary, his ever-present calm gave him a quiet, omniscience which made him appear much larger than he was physically. Ultimately, he was a man who, thanks to his skill and

Walter Riedel (1895–1974)

competence, was able to win the respect and confidence of the world around him.

As the eighth in the Riedel dynasty, he set a lot in motion in this difficult time of recession in order to keep his business from collapsing like so many others. He invested: Furnaces in the glassworks were equipped with the latest rotary grates, and production processes were partly or fully automated. He concentrated: The branch in Schatzlar (today Zacler) that his father Josef had bought in 1915 with its three glassworks was closed and eventually sold in 1930; as already mentioned, the textile subsidiary folded – affecting 600 jobs. He retooled: The works in Röhrsdorf (today Svor) were made more flexible in order to produce blanks for the optics industry, particularly for sunglasses and technical protective goggles. And he was innovative: As the technical genius of the family, Walter Riedel developed an opalescent glass that gave sales a new

At first sight not recognizable as glass: Lidded jar, vase and cup out of cut brick-red glass in simple elegance (around 1920)

boost. And hadn't there been money to be made a hundred years before with glass knickknacks like beads and buttons? He had new machines built for the fully automated production of spiral glass for bangles, as those colorful bracelets were called. Certainly, the competition was also producing mountains of bracelets, but Walter Riedel could now produce them with his special machines in excellent quality and at such low prices that the others didn't have a chance – he had left the competi-

tion more or less out of the picture for years. He also showed his virtuosity in another area, developing technical glass like monitor screens and prisms that were highly praised by specialists (and were used in World War II as prisms for tanks and anti-aircraft radar screens). The Klinger Company in Gumpoldskirchen, Austria, was also quick to make a deal with him to supply special glass for water level gauges.

Despite all these measures, things stayed tough

for the company. Riedel took over the production of red vehicle reflectors from relatives, which at first was a boon. Output quickly reached levels like the headiest days of bead production. But suddenly – practically overnight – he had to compete with other reflector makers. Instead of big profits, he faced losses, which he offset with his private funds »to keep the furnaces warm«. Giving up was not his thing. One had to be able to fight for markets.

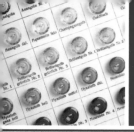

Delirious with Colors and Shapes

The earliest examples of glass from the Riedel Company do not come from museums or private collections but rather from excavations. Digging between 1973 and 1975 around the former glassworks in the Jizera Mountains that founder Johann Leopold Riedel had run from 1761 to 1775 turned up shards that could be traced to the artfully designed cups, carafes and liquor bottles from this old plant.

Museums like those in Jablonec and Prague have many well preserved Riedel glass products on display: Early 19th century clear glass cups with engraved shapes and ornaments, monograms, crests and vine decorations, some even bearing inscriptions.

The late 19th century offers particularly imaginative glass objects: Immense drinking mugs and delicate wine flutes from 1880, richly covered in images (featuring a pilgrim on the mug, for instance) and ornaments in bright enamel colors on light green glass; lidded tankards made of brown smoked glass or the Riedel-specific *annagrün* uranium glass with fused-on decorations painted in vibrant enamel and depicting allegories. Particularly pretty are the green wine flutes on which bunches of grapes were fused. Next to that, there are cups, *Römer* glasses, champagne flutes, bowls, goblets and beer mugs, all with lavish decorations and gold paint. But there are also other objects to see from this era: Busts and figurines from pressed, colorless glass that look as though they are made of ice. The effect is remarkable, like gazing at a frozen moment in time.

The close of the 19th century brings along some very special pieces: Bowls and vases decorated with bronze inlays and bronze figures. Beginning in 1900, glasses and vases featured delightful *Jugendstil* decorations on marbled glass. A particularly beautiful vase was presented at the Glasgow National Export Exposition in 1901. It is made of yellow glass with continuous blue casing inside and features an etched, gold-trimmed flower pattern.

The colors and ornamentation reflect a greatly pronounced creativity in glass art at the turn of the century: Engraved and painted birds of paradise on a colorless cylinder vase with lots of gilding or a cylinder vase with a radiant enamel peacock. Of particular note is a black basalt glass bowl with a reserved, opaque painted Japanese-style decoration. The era produced clear glass vases cased in violet and decorated with irises, lampshades in the same style, green vases with classicistic medallions with women's profiles in white enamel, vases in red, opaque glass rolled in mica, cased in topaz glass and gilded at the neck. Also to be admired are the opaque glass vases, at times brick red and at times marbled brown, with a vertical corner cut that gives a fascinating severity to an otherwise graceful form. Then again, there are vases that signal hedonistic or romantic passion with their vivid ornamental images. But bold and abstract creations were also produced, such as one black glass vase with a wire mesh casing and blue feet.

After 1900, the Riedel Company produced many high-quality table lamps with impressively artful combinations of decorations, bronze inlays, colors and forms – often classicistic or *Jugendstil*. Many lamps and lampshades bear the leaf patterns favored by Riedel. One piece in particular, a colorless vase with yellow opal inside casing and external

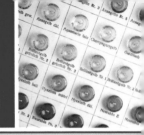

Glass lampshade beautified many turn-of-the-century middle-class homes: Shade shows a landscape motif, and bronze stand flanks an opal glass pillar

A typical Riedel decor motif: Mermaid with water plants and fish. Vase from 1926/7 has a yellow inner casing and a ruby red outer casing

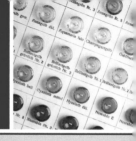

ruby red outside casing features a precious etching: A mermaid with billowing hair framed in water plants and fish. From 1920 there are free-blown vases and bowls in elegant, milk-white alabaster glass. The period also brought forth greenish yellow fluorescent cups, mugs, flagons, vinegar and oil bottles, even desk sets made of uranium glass, mostly with a corner cut to increase its optical effects. Especially appealing are the corner cut glasses made from the mystical looking antimony ruby and gold ruby glass.

The interior of the Czechoslovakian pavilion at the International Exhibition of Modern Decorative and Industrial Arts in Paris in 1925 boasted an especially made electric 2.65 meter high fountain of cut crystal glass, an impressive work that radiated an elegant weightlessness with its lighting effects.

From the 1930s, reflecting declining demand for beautiful and fine products as the threat of war grew, there are boxes with lids, liqueur sets, containers for toiletries, jars for preserves, flagons, pitchers, wall and ceiling lamps, and tea sets in crystal, smoked and rosaline glass. The glass now incorporated pronounced geometric ornamentation in its design. It also shows a new interest in very physical representations of girl and women nudes, usually realized in colorless or faintly tinted glass. At the same time, countless colors and shapes of glass buttons and bracelets were created. These knickknacks were the company's bread and butter like the production of victory, memento or birthday cups. In 1935, the Riedel Company led the world market in perfume bottles.

In the decor sketch book of the company Riedel Polaun, the mermaid motif appears as no. 81, depicted and colored

Skirmishes before the Apocalypse: Dark Clouds Gather over Europe

In December 1979 in Kufstein, Austria, Claus, the son of Walter Riedel, found a letter in his mailbox. Curious, Claus Riedel (9), opened the envelope – and it catapulted the new head of the glass company, who was now causing a sensation with his stemware, back into his family's distant past. Ernst Seidel, a former glassmaker who had once worked under Walter Riedel (8) in Polaun and even knew his father, Josef Riedel (7), son of the legendary Glass King (6), had written from Neugablonz (»New Gablonz«) near Kaufbeuren, Germany.

In one passage in his letter, this witness to history described how enthusiastic Walter Riedel (8) had been about technological innovations:

> When Herr Walter Riedel returned from his studies, he wanted even then to automate rod production. Furnace number five was the experimental furnace, the »iron glassmaker« as we called it. It was a one-pot furnace, raised up on an iron framework. When the tests started, he even brought in the Herr Father, Josef Riedel. It didn't work right yet. Herr Josef looked at what was going on and shouted, »Stop that! What am I supposed to do with all my workers? They'll all be out of a job!« He shouted even more loudly, »Stop it! This instant!«

Ernst Seidel went on to describe further experiences:

Herr Walter Riedel, your father, was a particularly reserved gentleman. He never raised his voice, despite the many worries his business brought him. In the good years, the Riedel Company had a daily output of rods and canes of 20-30,000 kilograms. These were years where reflectors were still pressed entirely out of glass. There was a daily production of often up to 10,000 kg of ruby glass alone, and orders had to be rationed. Unfortunately, the competition got stronger and stronger. Prices were being underbid more and more by the companies Kopal Münchengrätz, Breit and Fischmann Töplitz, and a lot of orders went to these rivals. Output fell to 4,000 to 5,000 kg a day. That brought serious economic concerns. By forming the Omnia cartel, they tried to shore up falling prices and share out sales according to capacities. Unfortunately, many glassmakers broke the agreements. Herr Walter Riedel tried to cover his huge losses with his own reserves. In this way, things went on and many jobs were saved. To this day, we hold him in very high esteem for preserving our daily bread back then.

Towards the end of the twenties, political conditions were changing more and more dramatically and hectically. In those times, the little man usually ran for cover. A businessman, however, could not. But even Walter was plagued by an uncertain fu-

The dream of many women: Toiletry set of pressed glass for the Riedel collection »Ingrid«, designed by Curt Schlevogt

ture. How could he know if what he was producing one day would be sellable the next, or whether the old distribution channels would still exist? On top of that, tensions between Sudeten Germans and Czechs increased in the 1930s, this made itself felt economically. Czechs who received state subsidies in the republic's heartland could produce significantly cheaper products and more aggressively underbid Gablonz prices. Sudeten German compa-

nies responded in turn with delivery boycotts to Czechs and with cartels – as Ernst Seidel clearly recalled. Whether he wanted to or not, as a leading business figure Walter Riedel gradually slipped into the role as the cartel boss and speaker for Sudeten German interests. The man who so gladly researched and experimented in his laboratory and knew how to utilize the results from it for his business in far-reaching ways now had to travel about, show his face in various organizations, make speeches and sit at meetings. The man who inherited his father's passion for technology could now no longer spend enough time with it. The man who valued bearing and composure and a more liberal outlook now had to come up with antagonistic, fiery words because the Germans of Northern Bohemia felt themselves threatened economically. Now the younger brother Arno had to take over more of the daily business. Arno helped his brother keep the company afloat, a simple Riedel tradition of being there for the family business, no questions asked. On the other hand, the brothers waged terrible arguments because Walter was not at all pleased with Arno's enthusiasm for the Nazis.

In his day to day business, Walter Riedel managed to establish a cartel to protect the rod making business, and as the last president of the chamber of commerce and business in Reichenberg, he secured the transfer of the export-dependent Sudeten German industry into the German economic sphere.

Amid all these relatively small skirmishes, no one could have seriously expected what an apocalyptic horror a certain Austrian was to unleash over Europe. The German *Führer* was becoming a more and more tyrannical monster. All the while, among the Riedels there still reigned the private calm which had always been in the past centuries: An intact world, quite cultivated, highly family-oriented, still patriarchal in the best sense, thoroughly self-confident but very distant from any pomp, circumstance and banal self-adulation. There were the servants, the tutors and the governesses. But they still stayed down to earth, for anything else would have been inappropriate and would also distract from the truly important concerns and tasks, which had to be attended to in order to bring success. Money – as every Riedel was aware in an unpretentious way – was there for a few pleasantries in life but mostly for the preservation and expansion of the company. Duties, tasks and goals were never neglected or forgotten. Responsibility was still written large. Walter Riedel from Polaun was, first and foremost, an industrialist.

One private pleasure Walter Riedel allowed himself and loved especially was hunting. He could talk about his chases for hours, and he spent all his leisure days stalking in the woods. Even members of the princely Liechtenstein family came from Vaduz to hunt with him in Schwarzental (today Cerny Dul). Schwarzental was a dream come true, finally his own hunting grounds, far from those of the nobility around Gablonz. He bought Schwarzental valley in the mountains of Eastern Bohemia from Jaromir Count Czernin in 1935 and had a hunting lodge built there based on his own plans. It was an impressive hunting ground with over 1,000 hectares of forest.

However, Walter Riedel did not just think of himself when it came to leisure and sports. Of course he knew that hunting was a fairly elite hobby limited to only a few people. Perhaps that was part of the reason he so actively supported winter sports in the Sudeten region. Without a doubt he felt a duty to uphold the Riedel tradition of social commitment. Indeed, the region produced some top athletes, like the world-class ski jumper Rudolf Burkert who won a gold medal in St. Moritz, Switzerland, in 1928. Burkert was among those Riedel employees whose route to work already provided a good workout. He lived in the higher seated

A very special glass relief: Two naked dancing women as lamp screen made of white opaline glass (after 1930)

Ober-Polaun (literally »Upper Polaun«), and when it snowed, he skied a slalom to work. The way home, uphill, also provided good aerobic conditioning. Over time, he tested all kinds of different secret recipes for ski wax, melting together ingredients like pig grease, birch tar and even recording discs. After all, he worked at a company that was always melting things together to come up with new products.

These were pretty fearless fellows who traveled

Walter Riedel had a big thing for skiing and supported local skiers. In the winter, many factory workers also came to work on skis

by ski. Some Riedel employees took part in a race they respectfully called the »Death Run«.

The book *Stolze Erinnerungen* (»Proud Memories«), a compendium of Sudeten German winter sports, notes:

The Josef Riedel Company offered in its way a unique athletic opportunity. Among the company bosses who played an important role as patrons of almost all the sports, gymnastic and hiking clubs between Harrachsdorf and Antoniwald, Josef Riedel of Polaun enjoyed a special standing. From »Herr Walter«, as Walter Riedel was always called, his »children«, as he called his sporting companions, could always expect the best advice which was also followed by deeds if they were necessary. For the times, the company offered them unique opportunities. The company owned and operated a ski jump in Wurzelsdorf that allowed jumps up to 40 meters and also a training jump for youths in Polaun. Adjacent to that was a slalom course; right next to it was a downhill slope with an altitude change of 250 meters that led from »Stöckl-August« through the »Vogelherd« and on to Tiefenbach. »Herr Arno«, Walter Riedel's brother, brought together everyone who wanted to learn to ski and was one of the first in the Sudeten area to teach the Arlberg technique. In the summer, this gold-medallist was a track and field instructor. The sports-friendly company also provided youths with access to a well-preserved building, the former glassworks in Klein-Iser [...]

Walter Riedel wrote the foreword for this book of recollections, and those few interesting lines from him make one ponder the stuff of which all the Riedels are really made, what attitude they needed to carry the glass company through the decades, through the centuries, and their constant succession of crises. For Walter Riedel this was a mixture of leadership qualities, high individual achievement and a pronounced team spirit. Walter Riedel in his own words:

In World War I, as a military ski instructor, mountaineer, infantry artilleryman and liaison officer for assaults, I frequently observed that individuals in a group of otherwise disaffected people can be excited by a cause and inspired to give their best. This experience taught me three things: First, that the proper selection, education, instruction and training in a subject can greatly contribute to an enterprise's success; second, that every person who feels individually spoken to faces issues of honor and does not want to disappoint; third, that well planned support, even in the background, can often achieve more than anything else.

While life seems to be business as usual, black clouds appear on the horizon that many people still could not, or would not, see. 1935, the year Walter Riedel bought his huge hunting grounds, was the year the radical Sudeten German Party won an unusual victory in the Czechoslovakian parliamentary elections. The party platform clearly called for the annexation of the Sudeten lands by Nazi Germany. The tensions between the Czechs and the German minority had become worse. One must realize that in multiethnic Czechoslovakia a Sudeten German victory was quite important: While only one percent of the country's population was ethnic German in 1964, in 1930 it was 22.5 percent; the 3.3 million Germans compared to the 7.4 million Czechs represented a more than significant share of the population. The remainder of the 13.9 million citizens of Czechoslovakia was composed of Slovakians, Magyars, Ukrainians and Poles.

As the Nazi party became more and more powerful in Germany, political events in the region were coming to a head. Walter Riedel tried to keep a calm demeanor, still going hunting and carrying in his pocket as always a few glass marbles with the latest colors to show them off to anyone who asked.

Postcard about the annexation of the Sudeten region by the »Grossdeutsche Reich« on October 1, 1938. In the foreground a bunker fortification in the Jizeras from World War I

And whenever he could, he spent time in the lab to create new, complicated technical glasses, for instance for specialized lamps. Walter Riedel was happy for those few hours. He continued to systematize colors in a big color index, kept finding improvements for working glass blanks and set up the fully automated production of compression rings, giving home workers many new forms for glass enhancement.

The world outside the laboratory, on the other hand, was getting bleaker by the month. As a world-renowned leader in the Gablonz glass industry with 31 red-hot furnaces, he got involved in more and more obligations that demanded his attention. Walter Riedel would have rather focused on his own work, but he hoped that his efforts in various committees had some value. He had a leading position in the »Central Association of Czech Industrialists in Prague«, the »German Association of Industry«, located in Teplitz-Schönau, the »Employers Association of Glass Industrialists«, which also had its seat in Teplitz-Schönau (today Teplice), and the Prague »Trade Association of Glass Industrialists«. He was also chairman of the hollow glass cartel, president of the Reichenberg Chamber of Industry and Commerce and president and chairman of various other associations and committees.

The childhood and youth memoirs of Walter Riedel's daughter Sabine, which she recorded a few

September 30, 1938: With baby carriages and backpacks, the Czech population fled from regions bordering on Hitler's Germany into the country's interior

years after his death, show that he regarded these activities more as a duty than as a calling. Sabine Riedel describes experiences, which demonstrate that Walter Riedel's villa was the manor of a wealthy man with servants, but that her father was a normal, caring person who was not particularly fond of big events. Soirées which brought high-ranking politicians and business friends into the Riedel home cost Walter Riedel a great deal of effort. Sabine Riedel relates:

> For big gatherings, even father had to change his clothes. He did it reluctantly and groaningly. But first a swig of raspberry schnapps from his old, cloth-covered flask, a canteen from the First World War. I can still smell that delicious scent, especially from when he gave me a kiss after a drink. The flask lay next to the tin Lipton tea boxes where, depending on the time of year, the winter or summer stockings were stored reeking of moth powder. On his dressing stand, Josef the butler had already carefully arranged the gold pocket watch, the white handkerchief and sometimes his medal on its chain. Now our services were required: We held his trouser legs as he got into his tuxedo.

What the family really valued can be seen in Sabine Riedel's observations about broken glass:

> My first experience with glass was biting into a Christmas tree ball. I was three years old and thought it was an apple hanging seductively from the tree. I felt blood flow from my lip and splinters in my mouth and got a good scolding. Even though we were surrounded

by glass, there was always scolding when glass broke. Glass is the result of the work of many hands and not a thing to be wasted, we heard. We learned to treat glass with care.

Notable in her recollections is how fascinated she was by the hands of this otherwise physically unremarkable man, hands that strongly expressed his inner being. For all the brainwork he did, much of his technological research remained, literally, handicraft. She writes:

When I think of my father, his hands appear to me. They were big, sensitive paws that had a powerful grasp but also held the most delicate glass rods in their fingers. I only felt them once on my little child's bottom, not so pleasant. It was good to feel his hands radiate on my back when I lay in bed with agonizing sunburn while Papa carefully spread the coolest salve in the world. He could just as tenderly lay on or take off chest compresses when we had colds. I see his hands cutting bread, chopping wood, sticking worms on fishing hooks, shaving, parting his hair, knotting ties, writing his signature, putting in the full stops »W. Riedel.« like a stamp, grasping a ski pole, firing a rifle in concentrated silence, dressing a buck without getting blood on his cuffs, holding a telescope in his hand while raising a grunt tube to his lips during deer rutting season. These hands were always warm, consoling, protecting; when a runny nose needed to be wiped, he immediately pulled the softest handkerchief from his jacket pocket. This handkerchief could also swab a gnat from my eye. The hands happily clinked around in his pocket to fish out well made buttons. They clinked uneasily with keys during prayers in the family crypt, expressing the deepest pain as they pressed a rose onto grandmother's coffin to say farewell. I can image how these dear hands, folded in his final resting place, found peace.

In the mid 1930s, Walter Riedel was still able to demonstrate his artistic skills at glassmaking, despite all his other affairs. One aspect of this was his work with the sculptor Jaroslav Horejc (1886–1983). Czech glass artwork owes many of its influences to this artist. His vases and glasses are counted among the best designs of the 20th century. In the mid thirties Horejc favored monumental glass reliefs, creating for the Palace of Nations in Geneva an eight-part relief with the theme »Earth and Man«. The relief had the astounding dimensions of 140 x 545 centimeters – and was cast in 1937 by »Jos. Riedel Polaun«; today it is in the Museum of Decorative Arts in Prague. Shortly thereafter, to the great ire of Northern Bohemian glassmakers, the Nazi government in Berlin issued various statements dismissing these wonderful works of glass as a *Mumpitzindustrie* (»junk industry«), stating that the German people had »more important tasks« to fulfill »than making costume jewelry«.

And in the time that followed, it became more and more difficult for Walter Riedel to give attention to his family, the hunt and the arts. On September 29, 1938, the prime ministers of Germany, Britain, France and Italy met and drafted the Munich Agreement. It prepared the way for Germany to annex the Sudeten territory because it stipulated the withdrawal of Czechs from the region. During that period, at the behest of several committees he represented, Walter Riedel had to conduct contact meetings in Berlin and Dresden with government and military offices. The political situation was extremely tense, and Arno once again had to run the company's business. Directly following the Agreement, the coming of the Second World War could clearly be felt: In the Munich treaty, the evacuation of Czechs from the Sudeten region was given a fixed timeframe between the 1st and the 10th of October, and right after October 1st, German troops occupied the area. On October 9, 1938, they marched into Gablonz and Polaun and were greeted by the German population with jubilation. Locals believed they had been liberated after twenty years of oppression under the Czechs. Walter Riedel was named chairman of the Sudetendeutsche Wirtschaftsgruppe Glasindustrie (»Sudeten German Glass Industry Economic Group«) by the Reich Ministry of Economics in Berlin and was later made chairman of the Bezirksgruppe Sudetenland der Wirtschaftsgruppe Glasindustrie (»Sudeten German District Group of the Glass Industry Economic Group«).

The War: Walter Riedel and the Agonies of the Secret »Tonne« Project

The shadows of war came closer and closer. Conversations at the increasingly rare evening parties in the lovely Riedel family villa revolved only around politics and economics. Walter Riedel (8) hoped that integration with Germany would bring a turnaround. Yet at the same time annexation by the German Reich meant a great danger for the company. After all, the export situation was going to change in the future. Ultimately, he was facing uncertainty and once again the prospect of uncontrolled economic and political eruptions.

When Hitler finally started the war, Walter Riedel – like so many others – at first did not regard it as a catastrophe. He could not imagine the dimensions Hitler's insanity would take.

Shortly after the beginning of the war, Walter Riedel began making fine, spin-able fiberglass for the production of rope wool. The glass threads were especially needed for technical insulation purposes. Not far from Gablonz, in Thuringian Haselbach, the industrialist Werner Schuller had developed a new method for spinning fiberglass without platinum, which was hard to acquire in wartime. On February 24, 1940, he received patent number 715884 for a »device for the generation of fine, spin-able fiberglass«. This technology optimized the machine speeds and glass fiber quality of existing methods. Officials were made aware of it, and the Ministry of Aviation recognized useful military applications for this material. It set things in motion for a joint venture between Schuller and Riedel. The two entrepreneurs, both used to being the »sole rulers« of their businesses, were not excited about this more or less coerced cooperation, but operatives of the Ministry of Economics locked them up together in a hotel room until they agreed on a contract. Later the men got along even better as they noticed they were made of the same stuff.

Riedel had now learned the true meaning of the word *Mumpitz* (»junk«). In times of war there was no demand for artful glass objects or charming little perfume bottles for women. Survival of the company rested on strategically relevant products. Jewelry, vases and carafes were now only being made in small quantities, making room for more technical applications of glass. The new production line began with lenses and prisms, especially for tanks, and was expanded to protective goggles for the *Wehrmacht*. Where glass blanks were once made for small articles, now badges for the *Winterhilfswerk* (»Winter Relief Organization«) were created. All in all, business was still running fine, thanks to Walter Riedel's continuing ability to develop new sources of revenue.

But Walter Riedel also initiated some things that might not have fitted in well with Berlin policy. The reports from Sabine Riedel's memoirs about the secluded mountain hunting grounds of her father indicate this:

123 · Feuerwehr Protektor W.Riedel

Walter Riedel is »protector« of the fire brigade. Without a uniform, the glass industrialist is distinct in the front row

My father wandered around his property for a long time to find the right place for his hunting lodge. As he conceived it, there should be a nice view, it should be protected from the wind and stand in the sun, and it should have a well nearby. The place he found was away from skiers and hikers, as also required, and had a spectacular view of the Bohemian lowlands. A water dowser came. A spring was found and tapped. Trees were felled, and construction started. A stout hit with a hammer, and the first stone was laid. »Stand firm, our little house« were father's words to dedicate the cornerstone. A box with the building deed and a few Czechoslovakian crowns was walled in beneath it. The house was built to match the landscape. With groundskeeper quarters, a bunkhouse wing for several guests, four bedrooms for the family, a living room, a kitchen and a stall for sheep [...] When the war came, the house became an invaluable hiding place for many people and things.

She does not elaborate on this »hideout«, even later in her story.

Walter Riedel attempted a great balancing act during the war. He wanted to preserve his life's work by all means. The company needed to flourish because it gave him a purpose in life, as it did thousands of other people, especially in the form of a decent job. On the other hand, he disagreed with many of the actions of Hitler and his followers, so he did what he could to help.

The new sales projections for modern fiberglass production put Walter Riedel in a confident mood. However, he still could not be sure if he could keep his company afloat with it. When the Reich Ministry of Aviation asked him if he could produce a 76-centimeter glass screen, he began to think. He knew that up to then no one had been able to and that the supplier at that time could only achieve a maximum of 38 cm. Walter Riedel (8) knew the screens would be used in anti-aircraft sighting devices and that the larger the monitors were, the earlier attacking planes could be spotted.

In fact, no one at that time thought it was possible to produce screens more than 40 cm across. The smaller problem – though it also could not be solved by any company specializing in picture tubes – still seemed to be achieving a quality good enough to produce a completely bubble-free glass of even thickness. The larger problem, however, was the perfect, successive cooling, or annealing, of the glass after its formation. Cooling glass too quickly caused stress – resulting in breaks. The larger the screen, the larger the stress factor. The manufacture of 38-cm screens had already produced a lot of rejects. The technical issue was tru-

ly intricate; large lenses today still require long annealing periods.

Riedel took a big leap of faith. Three weeks later, the man who had never shied away from a challenge showed up in Berlin with a stable 76-centimeter tube. To the astonishment of the military leadership it worked outstandingly. Riedel, the glass guru, the technical wizard, the modern alchemist, had a big order under his bet.

Shortly thereafter, he would have to pay for that with ten years of his life. At the end of the war, a trap closed on Walter Riedel, one he had unwittingly built himself with his remarkable technical prowess.

The end came for the company »Jos. Riedel Polaun« in May 1945. On May 8, the Russians marched into Polaun from the north, Czech partisans swept into the town from the south, and the wheels of the Riedel company came to a sudden stop. Walter Riedel received an order from the new Czechoslovak government to continue running the now nationalized company. Indeed, Riedel was one of the first companies to start up business and fire its ovens again. Though Walter Riedel had lost everything, and the entire family fortune was about to be nationalized – its value has been estimated at 100 million reichsmarks –, he would have immediately had an important task in the coming tough postwar period as a renowned leading developer, technician and company director.

But the fact that he was such a clever inventor became his undoing. On August 22, 1945, sixteen days after the US atomic bomb on Hiroshima, Walter Riedel, inventor of the amazing picture screen, was taken into custody. Apparently he had smelled trouble: The day before, he had tried to flee from the Soviet occupation zone with his wife and a valuable gold coin collection as their only possession. But his wife Claudia was simply not in the physical condition that day for a strenuous march. And so Walter Riedel buried the coin collection in his garden where the Russians later found it.

What exactly happened then became clear only many years later. Four years after Walter Riedel's death, a Rudof A. Müller wrote a letter to Claus Riedel in 1978. A newspaper article had made him aware of the Riedel glass company in Kufstein, having also mentioned the anti-aircraft monitors from that time. He wanted to report a few facts about the story of this screen »that are probably not well known« – and in fact must have remained unknown to Walter Riedel himself.

> The newspaper article only speaks of the large tubes for radar and television. But I would like to inform you about what was really going on [...] Back then it was me who negotiated with Walter Riedel and was the initiator of these programs. I am also a native of your homeland and come from the Jizera Mountains ... In August 1943, I was withdrawn by order of the *Führer* from the battle of the Orel bulge on the eastern front and sent packing to headquarters in Döberitz. There I was told that as a high vacuum technician with manufacturing experience I was being transferred to Fernseh-GmbH-Berlin-Zehlendorf [»Television inc., Berlin-Zehlendorf«] to

take over the management of the secret »Tonne« project. At the time, Fernseh-GmbH was the largest research institute in the area of high vacuum and television technology.

Due to bombing in Berlin, Rudolf A. Müller had the research facility moved to Ober-Tannwald (today Horni Tanvald). As head of the secret program – the planning of an extensive ground-based air monitoring system – he decided that he could no longer depend on the Fischer-Ilmenau glassworks, which had been the supplier until then, »because constant aerial bombardment had already reduced delivery to a minimum. Here is where the problem started that would have such terrible consequences for your father later.« Right at that moment came a »highest priority« order form the very top for large anti-aircraft screens measuring 760 by 540 millimeters.

The author of this letter at first tried to resist the order, not just because of delivery problems from the glassworks but also for another reason:

> Because I knew very well that no glassworks in Germany or Austria was able to blow a monitor tube more than 38 cm across because of the incredible pressure after evacuation. It is not yet possible, I thought, we needn't even try.

But Müller was told he had to because aerial defense was heavily dependent on it. He quickly thought of the respected Riedel name, first met with Walter's brother Arno, then was referred to company boss Walter Riedel himself. Walter said he would have to make a few tests first then confided in Müller that »the order came at the perfect time«. At the moment the company did not have »high priority« for its work, and he was worried his best experts could be requisitioned. Soon after that, Riedel called the head of the secret program and said he would take the order. Rudolf Müller continued:

Three weeks later the first 25 samples were delivered. Our test results turned out to be excellent. In the meantime, further orders had come from Berlin resulting in a total of 2,000 tubes by the end of the war. And it must be said that these picture tube cylinders measuring 76 x 54 centimeters were the largest that had ever been made in the world by then. Sole credit for that went to your father, Walter Riedel! Up to the end of the war we continued to work on them, and not a single one imploded during evacuation.

The letter from 1978 to Claus Riedel goes on, indicating that Walter Riedel had hoped for a swift end to the war and had been thinking of the future. He called Rudolf Müller once and indicated he would be willing to reduce development costs, if, Müller recalled, »we gave the company Riedel written permission after the war to include the tubes in its regular product catalogue under the name ›television glass‹«. Müller got this demand approved for Riedel, and the Riedel Company seemed to face a truly golden future in the coming television age. But it was not to be.

Eight days before the end of the war four Russian scientists came across the former head of the secret project in the Ober-Tannwald facilities: »We had already retooled everything for peacetime production. Then we were occupied by the Russians.« Müller had already hastily had his secretary »put a big, red X [on the big tubes] so that the Russians would think they were rejects and we could later destroy them to keep the tubes from falling into their hands. At the same time I burned over 2,500 patents and files on patents that were stored with us. But the Russians had apparently gotten wind of something.«

Because Müller spoke some Russian, he got along well with the scientists. With their help he was able to get some people he knew out of the Reichenau concentration camp. When he found out about the imprisonment of Walter Riedel in Reichenau, he immediately pleaded his cause:

With the help of Major Yarotzky, I was able to obtain a release order for your father. The Czechs were enraged when we came to Reichenau with Russian papers. I had driven there with two Russians and found out that your father was in Albrechtsdorf loading wood with a work crew at the Schowanek Company. We found him there, and he was handed over to us. That is, the Russians drove him home.

These facts had really been unknown until then. So Walter Riedel had been free for a time. Unfortunately, only very briefly. Then came a dramatic twist. Müller:

For the Nazis, the Riedel products are »junk«: Reinhard Heydrich (front group, right), Deputy Reichsprotektor of Bohemia and Moravia, in front of Prague Castle (August 28, 1941)

But when I got back to the facility, the Major said to me, »Your efforts were in vain. Orders from Moscow are that he must be brought to Russia immediately.« I couldn't understand it, since he had practically nothing to do with the really important armaments. We wondered about it for weeks until one day the mystery was solved.

I tried everything to get to Berlin. I wanted to know what had happened in the meantime with the devices we had deposited in a secret depot in Zehlendorf. The Russians didn't need to know this. I told our colonel I wanted to check where the caesium was that we had been keeping safe at »Fernseh«. Actually, I had already had those costly 25 kilos brought to the Black Forest by courier in the last days of the war. [Note: To give a sense of the value of caesium, today a gram of this silvery soft alkali metal fetches US $130.] But the Russians didn't need to know that either. I said it was still in a Berlin cellar. So one day they took me to Berlin to search and find the whereabouts of the caesium. A scientist, who had studied in England and the US for many years and who spoke pretty decent German as well, also came along on this trip. We had a very nice conversation on the way, and at one point I asked why Mr. Riedel had been taken to Russia.

The Russian scientist's answer showed the dimensions of what would cost Walter Riedel ten years of his life. According to Rudolf Müller, the former head of the secret »Tonne« project, the man answered:

> »I can tell you. It's very simple. When Berlin was occupied, they came across a flak tower near the zoo with a destroyed Jagdschloss FuG 218 location device attached to a so-called *Sternschreiber* or ›star writer‹. With this device one could locate any airplane taking off in England more than two meters above the ground and follow it with the Sternschreiber. And the bigger the picture tube was, the farther the device reached.
>
> When a Russian group reached the flak tower, the whole location device was wrecked, but the picture tubes on the Sternschreiber were still intact. In addition, the chief officer was a professional electrical technician familiar with this research. We Russians had also been working on a machine like that, but had to give it up because no one could make such big tubes. So when the officer in Berlin saw these tubes, he was really surprised to find such a thing and immediately reported it to the office in Moscow where he had once worked, and that's how it got started.« Müller concluded, »And just a few days later there was a warrant for your father.«

The letter from Rudolf A. Müller moved the Riedel family very much:

> One thing you should not forget, especially among experts: Within a couple of weeks,

In the 1930s, practical things are in demand: Part of a liqueur set with hexagonal base

Walter Riedel accomplished a technical achievement, without any fanfare, that the best and most experienced experts in all of Germany rejected as impossible. With picture tubes bigger than 25 cm, there were already complaints, and you could forget everything bigger than 40 cm. But your father managed 76 cm instantly. Things like that got forgotten in the chaos at the end of the war.

In 1956, the Americans were still struggling with tubes of that size. When I had a meeting in Buenos Aires in 1957 with the general director of the Corning Glass Works from New Jersey about altitude-resistant capacitors, his question was, »How did you make those big tubes during the war?«

Myself, I was able to escape deportation by the Russians because I took a big risk and had a little luck. In Bad Reichenhall the Yanks discovered me and wanted to bring me to the US by force, but I wasn't obliging. When the English tried to pressure me, I emigrated with my family to South America for fifteen years [...] Although I am officially out of the workforce, I still have a special place for the material glass in my heart because I am of the opinion that glass still contains many secrets that will continue to baffle scientists for years to come.

The letter to Claus Riedel (9) describes a moment in history from the days after the war in which many things took peculiar paths. German inventors, scientists and technicians lived in great un-

certainty. Some were lucky and got recruited by the English or Americans; for Walter Riedel, however, his work ended with deportation for a decade to the Volga and an Eastern Siberian camp.

While Riedel, in no way a war criminal, faced several dark years, two days later the American Department of War announced that all 400,000 German prisoners of war in the US would already be able to return home in early 1946. On December 4, 1945 – the Nuremberg Trials against the Nazi leadership had been on for two weeks – Walter Riedel was transferred from the camp at Reichenau to Russia as a »forced contractor« and forced laborer.

He did not know how long his deportation would last. At first he helped to rebuild Russian glass factories by contributing his knowledge, and later he worked in the laboratory of a glassworks as a developer and consultant. In 1950, when the five-year contract forced on him expired, Riedel finally wanted to return to the West. The Russians had other plans. At first they reacted with mild then stronger pressure and finally with threats to get him to sign an extension.

Riedel remained unfazed, stating clearly that he had fulfilled his obligation with the five years of work in Russia and now had the right to leave. Shortly before his work contract was supposed to have expired, he went to the Austrian embassy in Moscow. There he consulted with the ambassador, filled out formulas and had begun to discuss details of his return.

Apparently, however, the embassy was bugged. Riedel was arrested a few days later and accused of telling the embassy about his work over the last five years, making him a spy. As a result, he was sentenced to 25 years imprisonment and ultimately spent another five years in Russia, two of them as a forced laborer in Eastern Siberia. Because of the general easing of political tension after Stalin´s death and the great diplomatic efforts and work of German chancellor Konrad Adenauer for the prisoners of war, Walter Riedel was finally allowed to return home in 1955.

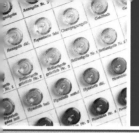

Moscow Special Prison No. 16:
Lev Kopelev Meets Walter Riedel

In 1950, when Walter Riedel was incarcerated in »Special Prison No. 16« near Moscow, commonly referred to as »Marfino«, he met a man who had grown up under the soviet regime of injustice. It was the Russian writer Lev Kopelev.

Kopelev, in his mid 30s then, went to prison because, after beginning life as a staunch communist and enthusiastic soldier, he had distanced himself from his previous behavior and expressed revulsion at the wasteland of humanity the Second World War had left in its wake. And towards the treatment of Germans in East Prussia. He was accused of »sympathizing with the enemy«. He later was a citizen of the world and champion for human rights and during his imprisonment he read German literature aloud to the German prisoners of war – Kopelev spoke German, a language he had studied at the university of Moscow.

The glassmaker Walter Riedel later did not talk willingly about his ten-year imprisonment, so traumatized was he by the time in Russia. He went to Marfino, after being sentenced to 25 years as a »spy«. It was described as a special camp for scientists and technicians, and Riedel stayed there until 1952. Kopelev had already been in Marfino since 1947 (he was released in 1954 after the death of Stalin) and worked as an interpreter for other prisoners – including Walter Riedel. He recorded his experiences from that time in his autobiography *Ease my Sorrows*. (»Ease my Sorrows« was the name of the church in the camp.)

Lev Kopelev recalls how Walter Riedel was making radio ceramics in a laboratory when they first met:

The lab technician Yevgeniya Vassilyevna praised him to the heavens: »You couldn't find a man like that in the middle of the day with a lantern. He only lives for his work. Always thinking out newer and newer combinations; he builds furnaces and he isn't too fine to get his hands dirty in the workshop. Always trying out new methods. Not a day passes without him improving something. He may be a capitalist, but he's such an untiring worker that our Stakhanovite workers could learn from him. Look at him: A skinny old man, you could blow him over, only his soul left in him, but tough at work. Sits down in the morning, back completely straight. At noon you sometimes have to tell him to go to lunch ten times. My other German, Fritz, is also hard-working, is also a capitalist, but he only plays second fiddle and obeys Walter without a word. He makes decisions, gives orders, and Fritz agrees, ›Jawohl, Herr Doktor, jawohl, sehr gut, Herr Doktor.‹

Yevgeniya Vassilyevna was not confident enough with her German and therefore called on me sometimes to translate new suggestions from Dr. R when they were discussed in the laboratory. And so I got to know him.

His gauntness made him seem larger than

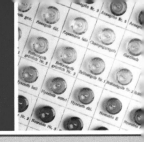

Former soviet major and later dissident and writer Lev Kopelev sometimes went on walks with Walter Riedel in the Moscow prison Marfino

he was. His narrow, pink, old-man's face showed hardly any wrinkles. He had gray, short-cropped hair, lively light blue eyes, a thin, firm mouth. He was rarely seen smiling, but he seemed neither sullen nor sad, just serious and concentrated. He spoke with a slight Austrian accent. In 1945, he had gotten a five-year contract and then worked in a large chemical laboratory near Moscow. He spoke respectfully of his colleagues and superiors there: ›Professor Ki-taygorodsky is a very good chemist. His foam glass is quite an interesting invention, offers a lot of possibilities. In the West he would have become a millionaire. He is a good chemist and a good person.‹

In 1948, Dr. R was able to find out his relatives' whereabouts: His daughter was in Vienna with her husband and his youngest son. The oldest son was living in Switzerland. Through his children he applied to the Austrian government for recognition as an Austrian citizen, having been a citizen of Czechoslovakia from 1919 to 1939, and he

143

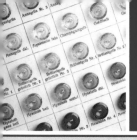

received confirmation. His contract then ran out in 1950.«

Kopelev relates the following story from Riedel about the extension of his contract:

»Professor Kitaygorodsky offered me a new contract for another five years. Then a higher superior came who invited me to see an even higher superior. They offered me better pay – five thousand instead of three thousand –, promised me new, better quarters, vacation on the Crimea, in the Caucasus. In the last five years, I had only had two vacations of two weeks each. I lived in the woods on the Volga in a decent little dacha, the food was good, and I could go fishing. But I hadn't seen my sons for nearly ten years, and I hadn't been together with my daughter and grandchildren for nearly five years […] I wanted to go to my family, and some financial problems needed attention […] Even the top boss spoke very politely to me but tried hard to persuade me: Just consider, think about it, you should really stay here because things will go well for you here, and otherwise you'll only harm yourself. I didn't understand. How could it harm me to return to my home and my family? […] The next day at work I was called out of the laboratory, and two officers brought me to the Lubyanka prison […] While awaiting trial, I was visited by another plainclothes officer, apparently a very important one because my examining magistrate, a lieutenant colonel, acted like a subordinate toward him.

This highly important officer again offered me a contract and work at the same lab. I refused categorically. He got angry and threatened that I was going to suffer […] I just could not believe the threats because I had not done the least thing wrong. I had honored the contract with hard work and had not broken any law. I was absolutely convinced I was in the right. They brought me to another prison. The officer on duty came with an interpreter and read my verdict from a thin slip: I was sentenced to 25 years for espionage. That was completely absurd! First of all, I had never spied in my whole life. Secondly, I was about to turn 60. How can they lock me up in prison for a quarter of a century? I wouldn't live that long […] Utterly absurd!« I helped Dr. R a few times to write complaints and petitions to the district attorney, to the Presidium of the Supreme Soviet and to His Excellency, Generalissimo Stalin himself. And so we developed – you could say – a comradely relationship. Occasionally, we took a walk together.

In his memoirs, Kopelev also quotes Walter Riedel's thoughts on the future of Austria. In 1947, he said:

I don't know what the new Austria will be like. I hope it will be neither red [socialist], nor black [conservative], and certainly not brown [Nazi]. I would like it multicolored: The old red-white-red and, in a new way, rainbow-colored. Monochrome is always bad, in art as in life, but for people and nations it is a great danger.

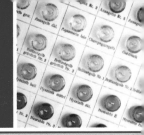

Prison camp in Russia: As a forced laborer technician, Walter Riedel had to share his knowledge with the Russian glass industry – for almost ten years

Confiscation after 1945:
The End of a Dynasty of Entrepreneurs?

With the Soviet Army occupation, Czechoslovakia was once again an independent state that incorporated the Sudeten region as well. In anti-German riots over 40,000 people were killed, and 750,000 ethnic Germans were forcibly expelled. On August 3, 1945, with the consent of the Allied Control Council, the Czechoslovakian government approved the expulsion of all Germans. For this relocation of nearly a quarter of the population, a presidential decree was drafted (part of the Benes Decrees, named after Edvard Benes, president of the country from 1935 to 1938 and again from 1946 to 1948), but the Potsdam Agreement rendered its passage through parliament unnecessary. The decrees, however, were implemented for the purpose of dispossession and revoking citizenship. One should not forget that German properties in Northern Bohemia, unlike in ravaged Germany, were real prizes. The whole region had been almost entirely untouched by bombs and guns throughout World War II, and all the German houses and factories could be taken over in excellent condition.

The Riedel enterprise was heavily hit by the wave of confiscation. There was nothing left of the Riedels in Northern Bohemia. Save for a few documents whose sober formulations record the beginning and the end of a two-hundred-year company history:

A handwritten tenancy contract, elaborately formulated in ornate, old-fashioned German, records the beginning of the Riedel dynasty in 1756.

Exactly two hundred years later, a couple of sparse, typewritten lines in a business registry, covered with official round and flat stamps, mark the dispossession after eight generations.

The huge bank assets, all of the companies and all private real estate accumulated after eight generations in the business were taken from the Riedel family by law in 1946 and transferred as state property to Czechoslovakia. The former owner of the largest glassworks in Europe, Walter Riedel, was now being forced to work as a contracted technician in Russia. The story of a great dynasty of entrepreneurs that had influenced the cultural history of glass, seemed to be on the ropes in 1946.

Many German companies ended the same way. Of course, Germany had started and lost the murderous Second World War, and now it had to pay. And of course, all of those lost material things are nothing compared to the immeasurably larger human suffering that visited the people of so many lands because of the cynical hubris of the Nazis.

But every person who survives terrible events refocuses his life afterwards in order to find his way again. He concentrates on what he is, what he was and where his world has gone, on the people and things around him. This is especially the case when the experiences are apocalyptic – and there is no other way to describe World War II.

The Riedels, too, tried to collect themselves after the roar of the fighter planes and the dull thuds of bomb detonations had finally passed. However, it was a fruitless task for a long time.

Family members had been scattered all about, and it was not until the mid fifties that they were successful, having found their way to Kufstein, where Walter Riedel spent his last years after being released from the Russian camp. One thing was clear to everyone: The company »Jos. Riedel« in Polaun, this vast business, was a thing of the past.

Even when fate becomes stormy, casting people about, perhaps into oblivion or perhaps to other, new places where they might take root again – one thing survives every crisis in almost unbearable austerity: Bureaucracy. With its laws, stamps, directives, signatures, files and registries it records facts in order to fulfill its task of ensuring that human society runs smoothly. However, these soulless records can never say what is really hidden beneath their file numbers.

Russian soldiers raise the flag of victory on the Reichstag at the end of April in Berlin. The Sudeten German region is again given to Czechoslovakia

And yet, in retrospect they often represent important historical milestones. That is the way the entries for the beginning and end of the company »Jos. Riedel« in the business registry of the district court of Reichenberg must be read.

Here is an example from the early days of the Riedel Company:

213/1 date of entry: 3 Mar. 1877. Company name: »Jos. Riedel«, location of main facilities: Tiefenbach, that of branches: Wilhelmshöhe, Wurzelsdorf and Maxdorf. Legal status of company: Public company engaged in glass manufacturing in Tiefenbach and Wilhelmshöhe, cotton spinning in Wurzelsdorf and flax spinning in Maxdorf. Proprietors are: Josef Riedel and his sons Hugo Riedel, Wilhelm Riedel and Otto Riedel. Each of them is empowered as independent signatories for the company. The company began on February 17, 1877.

And the official end of Riedel in Northern Bohemia is documented as follows:

213/46 date of entry: 18 Dec. 1945. Location of main facilities: Dolni Polubny (Unter-Polaun), that of branch: Pobr-Zacler (Bober-Schatzlar).
Comments:
1) By decision of the Ministry of Industry in Prague on 16 Oct. 1945, exh. no.: II-2-119.926/45 according to the Decree of the President of the Republic on 19 May 1945 no.: 5, the company will be placed under national administration. The provisional National Administrator, eng. Stanislav Bachtik, Professor of the Trade Academy of Mlada Boleslav (Jung-Bunzlau) – Kolonie 609/II, will independently represent the company with respect to the aforementioned decision and decree and sign for it such that under the company name he shall affix to his handwritten signature the supplement: National Administration.
2) The former name of the company location will be deleted.
3) The Czech name of the company location will be inserted.

213/47 date of entry: 16 Sept. 1946.
Comments:
By power of the announcement of the Minis-

After eight generations in Northern Bohemia, the president of the Republic of Czechoslovakia confiscated the entire Riedel estate by decree. The company name »Jos. Riedel Polaun« was expunged

try of Industry on 24 Aug. 1946, exh. no.: IV/9-243785/46 the appeal comment of the National Administration will be deleted because the company assets have been integrated into the newly formed national company Glass Factories and Refineries (Sklarny a rafinerie), previously Josef Riedel, National Company, Dolni Polubny (Unter-Polaun).

213/48 date of entry: 20 Oct. 1946.
Comments:
The entry of 16 Sept. 1946, no. 213/47 is corrected for legal purposes and reads:
1) By power of the announcement of the Ministry of Industry on 24 Aug. 1946, exh. no.: IV/9-240785/46 company assets have

been integrated into the newly formed national company Glass Factories and Refineries (Sklarny a rafinerie) previously Josef Riedel, National Company, Dolni Polubny (Unter-Polaun).

2) The legal power of the National Administrator expired only because these were assets which by announcement of the Minster of Industry on 7 Mar. 1946, no. 891/decision 1, section 56, part I/46 were nationalized.

With these few bare lines in a business registry, the 200-year-old entrepreneurial dynasty and 69 years of »Jos. Riedel Polaun« were brought to a close, the company name expunged and all assets confiscated by decree of the President of the Czechoslovakian Republic. The icy era between East and West began to run its course. The decree and the nationalization of assets rested on the simple and stereotypical widespread assumption that these came from invalid commercial dealings by »Germans, Magyars, traitors and collaborators« from the »era of subjugation«, meaning the enforced restructuring by Hitler in 1939 of the remainder of the Czechoslovak state into the Bohemian and Moravian protectorates incorporated into the German Reich, in which Czechs in these regions really had been oppressed and even terrorized. Because these people were declared »nationally undependable«, as it said in the postwar decree, all of their assets had to be placed under national administration.

While Walter Riedel was scraping by in Russia, his brother Arno was arrested and put to work in reconstruction and as a farm laborer in Czechoslovakia. In 1947, he was sentenced to seven years in a maximum security prison, found guilty of being a »tradition-oriented Sudeten German industrialist« – the sting of disgrace under the Nazis had left much raw pain among Czechs. Arno Riedel went to the infamous men's prison Valdice near Jicin. In addition to hard physical work, he had to provide his services to various chemical plants. After his release in 1950, he left straight for Germany where he worked in management at various glassworks.

The New Beginning: Wineglasses with an *Avant-garde* Design

»Hello, Sepp. Well, here I am!«:
After Escaping from the Train

Claus Riedel was freezing. The leap into the snow had completely drenched his thin, cotton prison uniform. He carefully raised his head. The train carrying other German prisoners to Bad Aibling in Bavaria had passed out of hearing. There he lay in the snow, surrounded by mountainous terrain, at his life's low point. He owned nothing but the skimpy clothes on his back. But even then he knew that what he had just dared to do was right. He had his freedom again – and himself.

On this sunny March 16, 1946, he began to trudge down to the valley, with a quick pace to keep from feeling his wet clothes. When he met a farmer along the way, he asked where he was. »Seventeen kilometers to Wattens« was the bent old man's laconic, slightly grumpy answer. Wattens! He could not have had better luck. Sepp, the cook in his unit, had once said to him toward the end of the war, »If things ever turn out bad, then come to me.«

Seven years before his death in 2004, Claus Riedel (9) related in a recorded conversation what happened after that:

Well, so I walked those seventeen kilometers. I didn't have anything, not a thing, no electric shaver, no toothbrush, no money. And I went to the man and said, »Hello, Sepp. Well, here I am!« I chopped wood for four days. It would have been unthinkable to live off the fat of the land and have food brought to me when I didn't have any money. Every day, Sepp went shopping down in the village in Wattens. I noticed that Sepp was looking at me skeptically, studying me. Finally one evening he said, »Listen, we're going together to go see an old gentleman tomorrow whose name's Swarovski. That's the founder of the glassworks here, and he wants to talk to you.« Well, I was incredibly nervous. Not because I knew who Swarovski was. It was the first time I heard the name. But I didn't have any release form, no papers. What if I fell into the hands of the police, or the French? The French were occupying Tyrol at that time. Anyway I was very uneasy. So we go down, go across the factory yard, and I see all these glass rods from Riedel they're using to press jewelry stones. Of course, I was amazed.

Claus Riedel recalled further:

Old man Swarovski was a handsome, lean fellow with a white, waxed mustache and a walking stick. He leaned on his secretary because he was blind. And then the blind man feels my face probingly and says, »You're a Riedel, you're Claus, and your great-grandfather was Josef. He was my teacher. Now I'll help you, because we know your father's in Russia.«
I was totally astonished. Swarovski called Manfred and Daniel, his grandsons, who were 30 years old then. He said to them, »So, now you have another brother.« Of course, they

had no idea what to do with me, but they kind of liked me.

Claus Riedel was given new clothes, got new papers and lived with the Swarovskis who had left Northern Bohemia many years before and set up in Tyrol to put a little distance between their glass-making secrets and the Northern Bohemian competition. Soon after that the Swarovskis told him, »We have spoken to the University of Innsbruck. You'll get 500 shillings a month from us. Go to the university and study chemistry.« Riedel was lucky again: »I came across a wonderful professor who gave me a really proper education in silicate chemistry, a great man that Professor Hajek.«

When his studies ended, he asked a Swarovski grandson, »Manfred, now that I'm done, can I come to work for you as a chemist?« The answer was: By all means, for he would be an asset.

Claus Josef Riedel (1925–2004)

That same evening, as all the Swarovski family members sat together, Manfred's »yes« was revised. Claus Riedel was told that they had not left Bohemia just to one day be imitated by someone from Gablonz. And that would unavoidably happen because eventually he, Claus Riedel, would surely get his glassworks back. Alfred, one of the sons of old man Swarovski, said to Claus Riedel in a friendly but firm way, »You would doubtlessly end up copy-ing us. For that reason we are going to release you back out of the family.« For his new start, the Swarovski family gave Riedel 100,000 Austrian shillings – about 7,000 euros.

Claus Riedel, by now married to the Italian Adia, whom he had met during the war in Liguria, moved around a lot with various jobs in the years between 1951 and 1956. First he worked in Naples, Italy, at the Cristalleria Nazionale for two years, then in Gelsenkirchen and Günzach, Germany, and then

The graves of the Riedel family in Polaun.

in Innsbruck, Austria. He learned the finer points of crafting drinking glasses, and also jobbed in other businesses – until he got a call from Wattens. Riedel should come to Austria immediately. There was something to discuss. The ÖVP (Austrian People's Party) Finance Minister, Reinhard Kamitz, who had headed the Reichenberg Chamber of Commerce with Walter Riedel in Northern Bohemia before the war, was concerned about a glassworks in Kufstein, which had gone bust. He wanted the Swarovskis to take it over because otherwise jobs for many Sudeten Germans would be lost. But the Swarovskis didn't want to because the production of stemware did not fit their profile. So they suggested Claus Riedel to the Finance Minister, as a professional up to the task.

Riedel, however, now fairly poor, said, »Buy a whole glassworks? How can I pay for it?« – »No problem«, the Swarovskis said, »we'll advance the money.« The deal seemed perfect, but fate once again had something else in store: Old man Swarovski died, and the family now had to pay around 22 million shillings inheritance tax (approximately 1.5 million euros). A loan for Claus Riedel was out of the question. But Finance Minister Kamitz did not give up. The glassworks absolutely had to be put back into professional hands. He interceded again and made an offer to the Swarovskis to reduce the inheritance tax due by the exact amount that they wanted to offer to Riedel as a loan. The deal was finally made to the satisfaction of all parties. With a starting capital of 4.5 million shillings (approx. 320,000 euros), Riedel took over the bankrupt »Tiroler Glashütte« from its previous owner. It was the historical beginning of what Riedel is today.

A year later, Walter finally came back from Russia carrying only a small bag. The former industrialist was now gaunt, exhausted, marked by ten years of coerced contract work and forced labor. But the 60 year-old was overjoyed finally to end this postwar chapter.

It was a moving moment in the mid 1950s between father and son, between the representatives of the eighth and ninth generation of the Riedel dynasty. They had not seen each other for sixteen years. Claus Riedel related, »I went to war when I was sixteen and really had only known my father up to that age.« At first, Walter Riedel lived with his son, and later the helpful Swarovskis pitched in. They arranged an apartment for him and his wife Claudia.

After ten years of reconstruction, the economy in many areas in Germany and Austria had picked up, and the people were beginning to show a certain prosperity. For Walter Riedel it was not easy getting adjusted to life after the long period of privation and intimidation. The son knew: »You cannot imagine how the man's mind was after so many years of prison. He was disturbed in so many ways. He couldn't even ride the train normally because he stood at attention for every conductor in a uniform.«

But Walter Riedel was too much of a Riedel to simply retire. His greatest wish was to build up a bead department; and he succeeded, too, with the help of an old foreman. In the meantime, Claus Riedel set up the »Tiroler Glashütte« as a top quality producer. His father was proud of what emerged. On the other hand, the many »contact points« of the two Riedel generations lead to many conflicts. It could not be avoided as both men had strong personalities, followed visions and wanted to pursue new things according to their own convictions. Walter Riedel was still attached to the idea of a glass factory with an extremely high output, while his son Claus, the ninth in the dynasty, purposefully sought success with fine glassware, the kind of aesthetic products that make people click their tongues in admiration.

The friction that constantly arose between the older and the younger generations in the Riedel dynasty due to their different views has to this day exclusively been regarded as a positive driving force, following an old motto: »Stoke the fire, don't save the ashes.«

Avant-garde in Glass:
Riedel Products with a New Philosophy

After the end of Riedel glassmaking in Bohemia – with the collapse of Germany in 1945 and the expropriation of the Riedel works in Polaun – a new direction in design was taken as glass production resumed twelve years later in Austrian Kufstein. Riedel was now intentionally no longer going to be a heavy industrial glass company, but rather a quality producer, specialized in fine, hand-made glasses.

Market opportunities, it was generally held, were only to be found with truly extraordinary pieces. And so it proved to be the case: Claus Riedel, the founder of the new company and the new line in glass design, was immediately successful. Unadorned, delicately smooth, very thin-walled, modern and without any ornate gimmicks, quickly diverged his glasses into two product groups: On the one hand the new minimalist and purist aesthetic of extremely thin, long-stemmed glasses (typical examples: Bruxelles, Exquisit or the Pokal hoch series), on the other the glasses from the Sommeliers series, uncompromising shaped to forms dictated by their different functions. The glasses from this latter series led the way for the functionally designed Riedel Gourmet Range.

Claus Riedel's very own first design – named Bruxelles – demonstrated the new direction: Simple elegance was called for at a time when most wineglasses were still quite heavy in appearance and feel. The perfection of the Bruxelles glasses gave a hint of the incredible skill the new design philosophy demands from glassblowers: To achieve these fine forms, they only have 50 seconds to blow a glass.

In addition to the remarkable wineglasses, Claus Riedel also designed other acclaimed products. His high-stemmed, mouth-blown candlesticks from 1959 were pure *avant-garde*, something experts have been quite happy to confirm. That same year Riedel was awarded the Austrian Staatspreis and two years later the German Staatspreis. This design is copyright protected in Germany until 2044. A bold design for a »television glass« from 1959 also received a silver medal at the Milan Triennale the next year.

The Exquisit glass series in 1959 produced another innovative first characterized by a high stem and an especially thin-walled bowl. The crafting of the stems and the particularly clear tone and elasticity of the glass have distinguished Riedel glassmaking ever since. Cups, plates and bowls were fashioned in a functional, clear and strikingly refined form similar to that of the new wineglass series.

In his 1961 catalogue, Claus J. Riedel displayed his vision of glasses specially made to suit different wines for the first time. The revolutionary concept followed the principle that the design is subordinate to the drink and its individual features. The concept distinguished Riedel more than ever before, because in the past, fads and fashions had determined the shapes of wine glasses, which would have a basic form that varied

The previous owners ran it into ruin, and then Claus Riedel took over the »Tiroler Glashütte«, today's Riedel Glass in Kufstein.

only in size (for example large glasses for water and red wine, small for liqueurs). The Riedel principle, however, is determined by completely different shapes and sizes, linked only by the designer's unmistakable signature. To this day, the gourmet knows one thing about Claus Riedel's work: That this kind of design succeeds in bringing more

pleasure to the nose and more enjoyment to the palate.

Worldwide recognition and many, many prizes – ultimately 28 – quickly followed for Claus Riedel. The starting point and quintessence of the new design philosophy was Claus Riedel's instantly famous Sommeliers series, which he

157

first presented in 1973 on the occasion of the founding congress of the Association of Italian Sommeliers (AIS, Associazione Italiana Sommelier) in Orvieto. It was the first gourmet glass series in the world and completely changed the world of wine. The clear, austere aesthetic and functional variety of Sommeliers became a source of identification for Riedel glassmaking in Austria.

It is no exaggeration to say that this glass series and its continuous further development and refinement not only changed the design of wineglasses for decades to come but can even claim a certain influence on the cultural history of wine. Riedel glasses, which are tailored to a specific wine like a finely tuned musical instrument, made it possible to appreciate fine wines more intensively and pleasurably than before.

The Sommeliers series consists of array of different glasses in a unified basic style, each style created for a very particular wine always in line with the company's principle »Form follows function«. The way a particular wine is made, from the pressing of the grapes to method of storage, right down to the physiological factors determining how it should be drunk determine the form of the appropriate wineglass. Volume, rim form and surface evaporation of the wine affect the design.

In his investigation into the way a glass can positively or negatively influence the taste of wine or spirits, he made one discovery in particular: All wine glasses up to then – with few exceptions – had almost always been too small. With this knowledge, thirty wine glasses were fashioned to guarantee maximum wine enjoyment. The Som-

meliers series alone was showered with countless prizes.

Later, in 1982, Claus Riedel's son Georg Riedel (10) took over wineglass development. He expanded on his father's findings and was creator of the »grape-specific« glass. Georg Riedel also brought mechanization to the Sommeliers concept and with »Vinum«, the first machined grape-specific glass series, he gave the wine-loving world a more affordable alternative.

Bowls and vases then re-entered the assortment in the new millennium. They radiated a refined charm, stylizing little-used decorations like flowers and grapes. The optically clear cut glass produced a commanding effect, particularly for vases but also for lamps and champagne coolers. Since the rebuilding of this traditional company, Riedel Crystal has been known first and foremost for making the very best wineglasses – best because they're functional.

Through Georg Riedel's targeted and persistent marketing activities, Riedel wine glasses also entered the important US market in the 1970s, further boosting sales. A particular milestone in the American wineglass market for Georg Riedel was an encounter with the winemarker Robert Mondavi on September 27, 1989. It confirmed his plans not only to supply this market, but to make a permanent mark by founding a separate company in the United States.

Today, in America as well, the name Riedel is immediately associated with the ultimate in wine glasses. The famous wine expert Robert Parker Jr., also known as the »wine advocate«, remarked, »The finest glasses for both technical and hedonistic purposes are those made by Riedel. The

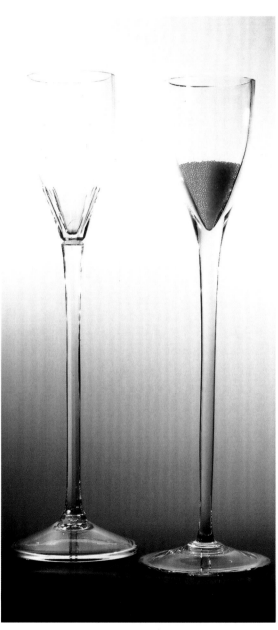

The »television glass« with an extended stem is a bold design from 1959. The next year Claus Riedel received the silver medal at the Triennale in Milan for it.

effect of these glasses on fine wine is profound. I cannot emphasize enough what a difference they make.«

Claus Riedel's legendary Sommeliers series set the standard for wineglasses worldwide and became the most successful range of wineglasses anywhere; as well as the basis for numerous innovations. As new wines entered the market, the development of glasses did not stand still. Georg Riedel intrepidly expanded his father's philosophy to conceive new drinking glasses, especially those for wine, to create an optimum taste experience. He paid particular attention to the development of the best wine glasses in all price categories, which he achieved with his machine-made glass series.

What determines the »technology« of today's Riedel wineglasses? An essential feature is the thinness of the glass, which belies its strength. The thicker the wine glass, the more the temperature of the glass affects the wine. If the wine glass is thin, on the other hand, the drinker can directly experience the recommended temperature of each wine.

All Riedel wine glasses are colorless, because in this way the visual aspects of the wine can be appreciated, its color, clarity and consistency.

The size, shape and rim diameter of the glasses are finely tuned, always with olfactory processes in mind. The pleasure of the bouquet is an important part of wine enjoyment – and it increases when the wine is swirled because, with more evaporation surface, the aromas can diffuse more intensively. However, human noses are as different as the grapes in wine, so both have to

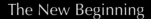
be correlated to some extent: With the right glass for a wine which places the nose in the right position. The diameter of the rim ultimately determines the tilt of the head when drinking; and ultrasound studies have shown that even the tongue takes different positions depending on the glass.

Designing and also producing a good wine glass is a science unto itself. Georg Riedel has continuously conducted a series of optimizing studies. For example, one analyzed how a sip of wine – a measure of measuring approximately 15 to 20 milligrams – connects precisely determined areas of the mouth, depending on the position of the head. The study took into consideration that the tongue has four zones with individual taste perceptions: Sweetness is tasted at the tip, bitterness at the back, and saltiness and sourness at each of the edges.

Various taste buds are addressed more strongly depending on where the wine first makes its most intense contact, and the sense of smell influences this as well. As the mouth is directly connected to olfactory nerves through the throat, we actually smell and taste at the same time, experiencing an integrated sensation.

In order to make this as refined as possible, at Riedel a wine glass is seen as an instrument. A twenty dollar violin sounds ghastly, but a Stradivarius, together with a good musician and a wonderful piece of music, may demonstrate the magic of the notes in all their facets. In this sense, a Riedel glass is conceived like a Stradivarius to achieve the highest level of resonance, harmony and enjoyment.

Naturally, even the most perfectly formed wine glass cannot perform miracles, can't turn a sour Riesling into a fine wine. But it highlights perfectly a wine's characteristics and thus does bring improvements to it. In this way, for example, a functional wine glass does not emphasize the bitter qualities of tannin-rich red wines acutely or astringently, but rather in a pleasantly round way, balanced with fruitiness. When wine is poured in two different glasses, you can already notice a difference in the smell: An aroma can differ so much that it is hard to believe it is one and the same wine.

The Sommeliers series drew all these findings together and put them into practice. For each new glass that is produced, there is an exactly predefined goal: If, say, tannin is to be de-emphasized – as it is the case with full-bodied red wines of medium acidity with high tannin levels like a Cabernet Sauvignon – then the glass has to achieve this. There will be experiments, researches and tests until that goal is finally reached. The task is always different: For a Pinot Noir, for instance, acidity should be balanced, but for a Chardonnay it should be highlighted; for light Riesling, the task for the glass form is not to emphasize the high acidity but rather make its mineral aftertaste, or »finish«, clearly perceptible.

The Riedels of today – meaning the epoch after the end of World War II with Claus Riedel (9) as the company's re-founder in the fifties and with Georg Riedel (10) and Maximilian Riedel (11) as the designated successor and current CEO of Riedel in the US – have dedicated themselves to the advancement of wine culture and have greatly influenced its development for decades. Their

Bruxelles is Claus Riedel's very first design (1957) after the resumption of the dynasty in Austrian Kufstein. Bowl and stem are produced from one piece

passion for the subject extends to minute details. This can be seen in the following excerpt from the Riedel Sommeliers Guide:

A colorless, unadorned glass is needed in order visually to appreciate a wine and assess its color, clarity and consistency. A thin-blown bowl means the temperature is immediately felt. Thick walls have the disadvantage of transferring the temperature of the glass to the drink. Swirling wine in the glass heightens the pleasure of the bouquet. Enlarging the evaporation surface area increases the variety and intensity of aromas. Scents are best experienced by bringing the nose into the correct position from which it can search for the message of the wine deep in the center of the glass.

Now we are ready for the first drink! Wine and, particularly, high-alcohol beverages are drunk »in sips«. It is this fact that makes it possible to guide a drink with a glass. Bringing a glass to the lips requires the subconscious coordination of the head and body. The size and shape of a glass provide the basic information for the body's posture, whereas the diameter of the rim determines the head's position. Ultrasound studies have shown that the tongue also takes different positions depending on the glass form!

It is first the lips that sense the nature of the rim and the thickness of the glass. With a slight backward tilt of the head, the flow begins. Controlled by the form and rim, a »drop« of 15 – 20 grams covers an exactly determined area of the mouth. The viscosity and temperature of the drink are transmitted by touch, and shortly after that the taste begins to develop. The tongue and its taste receptors can only distinguish four sensations, sweet at the tip, bitter in the back, and salty and sour on the sides. Depending on the form, size and rim diameter of a glass, the body, head and tongue take up a specific position. Thus, it becomes possible to position a sip exactly in order to activate specific taste buds. The intensive, multifaceted flavor sensations then only emerge in combination with the bouquet. The mouth is connected to the nose through the throat, so we smell and taste at the same time. Fruit, acid, tannin and alcohol are the variable flavor components of a wine that a glass transmits. As an instrument of drinking pleasure, the glass is responsible for the harmony and balance of these components. When tasting wines, whether dry or sweet, the interplay of fruit and acid on the tongue is very important. With the right glass, they can be harmoniously attuned to each other.

Swallowing the wine immediately would reduce the pleasure, which is why the wine is swirled again in the mouth to address all the flavor receptors. Some people pucker their lips to inhale slightly, mixing air with the wine and experience the flavor more intensely. Finally, swallowing and the finish it leaves determine the quality and enjoyment. In this way the bitterness of a high-tannin red wine can be experienced differently through the transfer medium of the wine-glass. The flavor profile of the same wine in different glasses can emerge anywhere from pleasantly round and fruity to vegetal, harsh and astringent. Even the wine's finish on the palate is the result of complex mechanisms of the body that are determined by the glass's form.

A resumé of the Riedel glass philosophy can be formulated as follows:

Function and enjoyment put to the test – wine tasting speaks to all the senses:
Sight: The first contact with the drink, like a wine's color, but also the visual effect of the glass.
Touch: A Riedel glass should always be picked up by the stem. Feel the perfect balance of the glass. Handcrafting guarantees the silken surface of the stem, foot and bowl.
Smell: In order not to falsify the characteristics of the wine, it is necessary to match the form and volume of the glass to the character of the drink. The intensity of aromas is increased by swirling the glass. The olfactory details of the drink are better sensed. Your nose decides your personal preferences for different wines! Your olfactory sense is able to define several hundred aromas. The quality of a fine wine is apparent particularly in its bouquet. Take a conscious pleasure in this experience.
Taste: This usually confirms what your nose has already sensed. Form-specific parameters affect how the drink arrives in the mouth and how it subsequently develops its quality there. The form of the glass, its volume and the diameter of the rim (including its finish, whether rolled or cut) direct the sip (narrow or wide – front or back) to the tongue, which senses the four flavor components – sweet, sour, salty, bitter – depending on its sensitivity. With the tactile sense of the tongue we are able to sense the temperature and consistency of the drink. The wine unfolds further on the palate, but the taste intensities of fruit, acid and tannin are expressed completely differently in different glass forms. Even the finish is heavily influenced by the form of the glass. The right glass leaves the mouth with a pleasant memory, eagerly awaiting the next sip.
Hearing: Glasses can't speak! But they do sound wonderful when you touch glasses for a toast. Make sure you don't touch glasses at the rim or the foot, but rather at the widest point (»cheek to cheek«).

The Riedel glass philosophy and the portfolio of diverse products resulting from it are most vividly illustrated by the history of individual glasses, for example the Tinto Reserva and Burgundy Grand Cru. Although both glasses are intended for fine red wines, they differ greatly in concept and form.

Riedel describes its Tinto Reserva in this way:

Tempranillo is the most famous grape variety on the Iberian Peninsula. Riedel has actually devoted not just one, but two different glasses to Tempranillo. After a protracted, highly meticulous testing process which involved three major tastings between late 1997 and late 1998, it became apparent that Tempranillo presented some of the same challenges as another »chameleon« grape variety, Syrah. Younger, less extracted, less tannic, more floral types of wine made with Tempranillo behave in a markedly different way from more tannic, oak-aged barrique wines such as the top Gran Reservas from Ribera del Duero or Rioja. The three successive panels of Spanish tasters, which included such major growers as Pablo Alvarez (Vega Sicilia), Alejandro Fernández (Pesquera) and the Marques de Griñon, appreciated the general shape – wider bottom, narrower mouth – that has been so successful in Riedel's Hermitage glass. But they came to the conclusion that a smaller size accommodates young Tempranillo's voluptuous aromatic qualities perfectly, while a larger liquid volume is preferable in order to highlight equally the flavors and finish of the top oak-aged Tempranillo wines, with their fine tannin structure. Therefore, the final panel, including the top Bordeaux winemaker Michel Rolland, who actively works with Tempranillo in Spain, unanimously recommends a twin solution to suit both styles of wine perfectly, after testing the top glasses developed from prior panel sessions. There is a smaller Tempranillo glass produced in the Vinum range, and a markedly larger (but identically shaped) Tempranillo Reserva glass in the Sommeliers range.

Georg Riedel relates the following about the Burgundy Grand Cru glass:

This glass was described by *Decanter* magazine as »the finest Burgundy glass of all time, suitable for both young and old Burgundies«. Its shape, developed in 1958, represented a quantum leap in terms of wine glass design – and has earned it a place in the permanent collection of the New York Museum of Modern Art. This »beautiful monster« of a glass can take apart a lesser wine, mercilessly showing up its weaknesses. But a great wine – a top-class Burgundy, Barolo or Barbaresco – will be revealed in all its glory. The large bowl allows the bouquet to develop to the full, while the slightly flared top lip maximizes the fruit flavors by directing a precise flow onto the front palate. Certain wines and grape varieties require this type of controlled delivery. By ensuring that the fruit is highlighted while using the marked acidity of the wine to keep the flavors in balance, this is a glass that produces a superbly three-dimensional »taste picture«.

This intensive study and development, however, was not limited to wine glasses. For the product diversity of the oldest European glassmaker, it was only natural to produce the perfect glass for other alcoholic beverages, too, whether they be port, sherry, cognac, tequila, raspberry brandy or aquavit. In most cases, consumers are surprised to discover that Riedel glasses look completely different from the classic glasses for each beverage. For

A revolutionary concept: The world's first gourmet glass series Sommeliers (1971), designed according to wine-specific criteria. It ensures optimal wine enjoyment

example, Riedel threw out the old, balloon-like cognac glass because its evaporation surface is much too large, only emphasizing the harshness and alcohol level.

Also unusual is the form of the single malt whisky glass, not the heavy whisky tumbler with a thick, flat base but rather – completely unusual for a whisky glass – a small, relatively delicate, thistle-shaped glass with a truncated stem. Its basic form is cylindrical, narrow with a stem base and a very steep, flared lip which directs this quality liquid to the point in the tongue that activates the relevant taste zones. This perfectly highlights the typical features of malt whisky.

Georg Riedel commented on the creation of this still very new glass in which a good single malt can be a revelation just by virtue of its bouquet:

One day, Campbell Distillers from the Scottish Highlands invited me to design a glass for their single-malt whisky Edradour and Aberlour. Single malt, you should know, is a drink with individuality, made with years of tradition and ripened in oak casks of different origins. Highland, Lowland, Islay and Irish malt whiskies are made 100 percent from barley which greatly influences the whisky's personality. Certain glasses are necessary in order to emphasize perfectly this barley character. Mostly cup-like glasses are used that don't do justice to its various nuances. The Scots swear that adding a splash of water highlights its aroma better. Thus, the goal was: Riedel's single malt glasses had to achieve this effect without »watering down« the concentration.

Riedel discovered that a slender, high form softened the harshness of the alcohol. For the fine-tuning, a range of prototypes were made that varied in diameter and height. The outturned lip was chosen in order to emphasize the fruit and to remove the sharpness of the alcohol. The fine-tuning took place in the Highlands at Aberlour. From the various possibilities a single form was chosen as absolutely ideal by both the master distillers and the managers at the whisky distillery. It brings out the sweetness and the creaminess of a single malt. Only in the finish does this new form reveal the strength of the alcohol.

In September 1992, the revolutionary malt whisky glass also survived its baptism of fire, at a tasting with a panel of professional experts in London. In a blindfold test, four excellent single malt whiskies were tasted in four different glasses. It was obvious that in the traditional whisky tumbler, the subtle flavors of single malts were simply lost, that a brandy balloon overstated the alcohol at the expense of the fine aromas, and that the standard copita tended to magnify imperfections while flattening flavors. The clear victor was the new Riedel whisky glass.

In summary: Although they are doubtlessly beautiful products, Riedel glasses are not just designed for their visual qualities. The professional eye of the designer is no longer enough. The most important measure is the principle »Form follows function«. Enthusiasts and experts appreciate it: The development of the single malt glass was –

next to his achievements in the design and manufacture of wineglasses – a primary reason why Georg Riedel was named by Colin Parnell, editor-in-chief of the British trade magazine *Decanter* as »Decanter Man of the Year« for 1996. Parnell was involved in the development of the new glass and thus aware of what an achievement it represented.

Message in a Bottle:
A New Glass Aesthetic Causes a Sensation

On March 3, 1957, one of the oldest glass families in Europe took up production again after an enforced 12-year pause. The new Riedel Company in Kufstein improved from year to year. Claus Riedel's concept of a pure form transposed into highly aesthetic thin-walled wine glasses, was a bold statement at a time that seems to have suffered occasionally from egregious delusions as far as good taste was concerned. One need only think of the thick Scandinavian glasses on twisting kidney tables or bulky hardwood tables. They were the height of fashion. But Claus Riedel was not a slave to fashion, had his own head and – influenced by *Bauhaus* and the styles of architects like Josef Hoffmann and Adolf Loos – thought in terms of synthesis, wanting to combine the technical with the aesthetic. Many people later said he was practically obsessed with glass.

The breakthrough came when experts praised the design of the Sommeliers series, gourmets recognized how much better their favorite wines tasted in these finely balanced glasses, and politicians and actors drank from Riedel goblets at big events. Among this wine glass *avant-garde* were Winston Churchill and the Duchess of Windsor who swore by these new Riedel creations. Claus Riedel stated later that he saw many developments as preordained: »My divine intervention began with the leap from the train into the snow cornice. From that point on I felt I was guided by God. That I was led to Naples to learn how to make drinking glasses and that fate *assigned to me* the glassworks in Kufstein, that I then made, by creating the Sommeliers series, drinking glasses there, that's divine intervention – it can't be anything else. It was fate that led me. Man proposes, God disposes.«

What Claus Riedel described as God's will, was a sensation. In 1969, after more then ten successful years, a second glassworks was opened in addition to Kufstein – the Claus Josef Riedel Glashütte Schneegattern GmbH in Upper Austria. A state of the art mouth-blowing production facility was built at Schneegattern. An important friend and early associate of Claus Riedel was Rudolf Trawöger, who worked as draftsman, designer and implementer. He brilliantly put the glass forms Claus Riedel envisioned to match the character of different grapes to paper. He developed exact drafts that were then transformed into the prototype wooden molds.

Where Walter Riedel was a genius as a technician, Claus was as a designer. At that time no one had the idea of creating a wine glass with a volume of over a liter. The hobby sailor and enthusiastic car and motorcycle driver had become so respectable as a designer in the sixties that a fruitful cooperation with the Rosenthal company was formed. Riedel was often involved in their designs, creating his own or improving ideas from other designers. He often said, »We're talking about function and must know that aesthetics are not enough for a design.« He was also the first

Moonstone inspired Claus Riedel to rethink the basic materials of glass (Apollo 11 with Edwin E. Aldrin and Neil A. Armstrong; photograph from July 20, 1969)

one to speak of the »glass transmitter« which transforms the smell and taste of wine. Claus Riedel proudly demonstrated to great acclaim what that transmitter can achieve at public wine tastings.

Excerpts from a 1963 letter from Philip Rosenthal to Claus Riedel show how new prod-

ucts arose in this cooperation through lively communication:

[…] a young man just came from Amberg and brought me your concept designs for place plates and the vase »Seltene Erde«. My dear Mr. Riedel, I think your

Wie die „Tiroler Tageszeitung" bereits meldete, überreichte Prof. Claus Josef R i e d e l anläßlich der Errichtung eines mexikanischen Konsulates in Innsbruck Konsul Manfred S w a r o v s k i die erste der 300 vom Mexikanischen Olympischen Komitee bestellten Vasen, die das offizielle Geschenk des MOC während der Olympischen Sommerspiele 1968 in Mexiko sein sollen. Die Vase ist jener Säule nachgebildet, die das riesige Flugdach des anthropologischen Museums in Mexiko-City trägt. Dieses Museum ist ist eine Gründung des mexikanischen Botschafters in Österreich, Ihrer Exzellenz Amalia de Castillo L e d ò n.

„Mexikanische Olympiavase" wird in Kufstein erzeugt

Die Säule trägt verschiedene Symbole, die in genau derselben Anordnung auf die Vase übernommen wurden. Wir geben nachstehend drei Skizzen der Vase wieder, auf denen die einzelnen Symbole gut zu erkennen sind.

● 1 und 2 stellen Jaguar und Adler, alte traditionelle Indianersymbole, dar.

● 3 zeigt ein Schwert, das darstellen soll, Mexiko sei lange Zeit infolge Stammesfehden geteilt gewesen. Über dem Schwert steht aber schon die aufgehende Sonne der Einigung, die nicht zuletzt aus der starken Völkervermischung kommt. Bekanntlich sind die Mexikaner stolz darauf, daß sie als Ganzes einer Vielfalt von Völkern entstammen.

● 4 zeigt die Indowurzel und 5 die Spanierwurzel.

● 6 ist das gemeinsame Herz und mit

● 7 ist der siegreiche Gott des freien Mexiko zu verstehen, der aus der Vereinigung von Indianern und Spaniern emporwuchs.

● 8 ist das Symbol weiblicher Fruchtbarkeit und der Vollständigkeit. Hier ist die Sonne nicht mehr — wie noch unter 3 — vom Schwert geteilt. Die halbe Sonne ist das Zeichen der Vollendung.

● Die Alraune, 9, ist das Zeichen geistiger Fruchtbarkeit.

● Zum Symbol 10 hin verbreitert sie sich gewaltig nach allen Richtungen der Windrose, und unter

● 11 ist die Bedeutung dieser Geistigkeit Mexikos für die ganze Welt symbolisiert.

● Symbol 12 zeigt den freien Mexikaner, über dem der Adler der Freiheit schwebt. Links ist der Lorbeerstrauch, rechts die Kornähre als Symbole der Ehre bzw. der agrarischen Fruchtbarkeit des Landes widergegeben.

● 13 bedeutet den durch Stammesfehden verwundeten Körper Mexikos.

● 14 ist das Symbol für den Krieg gegen die Vereinigten Staaten von

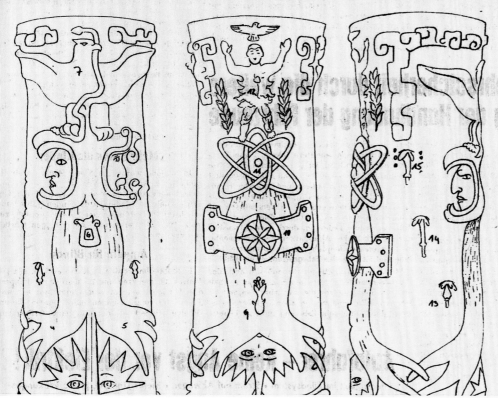

Honorable commission: Claus Riedel designs a vase for the 1968 Summer Olympics in Mexico. Modeled on a pillar with Mexican symbols

place plate idea is excellent. It's really like you said, a very new idea [...] I'm thrilled! Now I'll take the things to Mr. Rosenthal on Monday and will give you any news right away. Best regards [...]

Claus Riedel became an increasingly sought-after designer. Many companies wanted his creative input. In a letter from 1969 – as the German economic miracle boomed – the Thomas Glas und Porzellan AG, which also belonged to Rosenthal, wrote to Riedel:

Dear Claus, we have made the first samples of the pantograph glass and find it very attractive. It's convinced us [...] Please don't make the champagne glass too small. We're suffering partly from champagne glasses that are too small and they are giving us a reputation as water drinkers.

Rosenthal wrote excitedly in a press release from 1970 about the designer Claus Riedel:

Good, glass-friendly forms are not enough for him; his glass has to be functionally designed, too. Riedel's designs are also notable for their remarkable certainty in taste. He knows the potential but also the limits of glass. In search of new forms of expression, he does not rely on experiments or accidents but instead prefers systematic development. What Riedel designs are true innovations, as beautiful as they are usable. The forms of Riedel glasses are never for their own sake. You can always recognize – even in these avant-garde designs – the function around which the whole concept revolves.

Numerous international prizes for design distinguished Riedel from its competitors. It is an impressive list of selected awards that Claus Riedel received, even in his first years at the new Kufstein Company:

1958: Grand Prix at the Brussels World Fair for the glass sets Bruxelles and Exquisit

1959: Austrian Staatspreis

1959: The Corning Museum in New York names the Exquisit the »Most Beautiful Glass in the World«. It is chosen from 1,824 glass creations from 173 makers in 23 countries and today stands in the Museum of Modern Art in New York

1960: Three silver medals for Riedel glass at the Milan Triennale

1961: German Staatspreis at the Munich Handwerksmesse

1962: Austrian Staatspreis for the glass set Burg

1964: In connection with the Winter Olympics at Innsbruck Claus Riedel receives a commission for a representative gift: He designs a crystal piece that suggests ice and bears the city seal of Innsbruck using a new engraving technique. The piece is awarded a gold medal at the Milan Triennale

1966: The American Institute of Interior Designers gives Claus Riedel the International Design Award for »Glass. Design and Manufacture«

1969: The glass Monaco 283 is awarded the German Bundespreis »Gute Form«

1970: The vase Samenkorn is distinguished with the »Premio Internazionale Vicenza«

An honorary title as professor was granted to Claus Riedel in 1965 by the Austrian president and Ministry of Education in recognition of his achievements as a manufacturer and designer. It made him Austria's youngest professor, and from then on he was often casually called the »glass professor«. At that time, he was also vice-president of the Österreichisches Institut für Formgebung (Austrian Institute of Design). In 1975 Claus Riedel further received the *Grosses Ehrenzeichen für Verdienste um die Republik Österreich* (»Grand Decoration of Honor for Services to the Republic of Austria«), in 1980 an honorary membership to the Corning Museum of Glass in New York, in 1987 an honorary doctorate from the University of Miami, and in 1989 the *Grosser Kulturpreis* (»Grand Culture Prize«) from the Sudeten German Landsmannschaft. In its letter of praise, the group wrote, »Claus Josef Riedel truly offers the best example of how, under the most difficult conditions, a great and traditional legacy can be taken up, successfully continued and – above all – creatively reinvented«.

Still in the sixties, Claus Riedel (9) was granted an especially honorable task: He was commissioned by the National Olympic Committee of Mexico to design a vase for the 1968 Olympic Games and to produce 300 of them. The vase was later presented as an official gift to special guests at the games. Riedel created a vase based on the column built by the architect Ramirez Vázquez that had become a world famous landmark as the calling card of the Anthropological Museum of

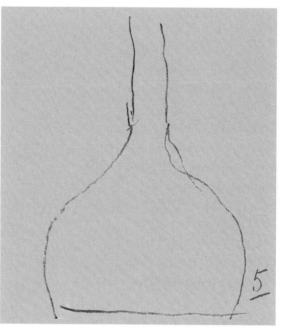

New products are created in cooperation with Rosenthal AG. Claus Riedel often sketched his visions with rough lines

Mexico City. It was shown to the public for the first time on March 2, 1968, at the opening of the Frankfurt Messe. The object, kept secret up to then, was a true work of art. Like its larger model, the museum column, the vase incorporated ancient Mexican symbols. A sword flanked by a jaguar and an eagle represented the old tribal feuds, above which shined a unifying sun. Branches with a common heart symbolized the mingling of Spanish and native origins. A mandrake was emblazoned on the other side of the vase as a sign of fertility. Other symbols were used that Riedel did not simply copy from the column but rather fashioned in individual designs. The gift for Olympic visitors brought its creator great acclaim.

A vase like ice: With the city seal of Innsbruck, the Olympic Committee had an impressive gift of honor for the 1964 winter games

As carefully as Claus Riedel considered aesthetics, as committed and creative as he was with glass design, he had a loose approach to other, equally important areas of the company. He once said he did not need to understand accounting, since he could hire an accountant for it. The result was that in the 1970s, while the company's image rose, internal financial problems emerged. Claus Riedel was then fortunate that his son Georg, who by then was working at the company, had a sober, analytical eye and immediately spotted the weaknesses in the corporate structure. As his measures were successful and his emergency brake worked, Georg Riedel began to expand his influence to get more say in the business. Georg Riedel made all the right decisions. His level-headed approach, self-confident leadership and the new

above: The first epochal glass set: »Grand Prix« at the Brussels World's Fair in 1958, named »World's Most Beautiful Glass« in 1959, »Medal for Exemplary Design« at the 12th Milan Triennale in 1960

right: Timelessly beautiful: The Samenkorn vase from 1964

directions he has taken with the company – based on his father's core product lines – have led Riedel Crystal to the stability that the company enjoys today.

How Beautiful Design Can Bring True Pleasure

Design enchants, creates a mood, enhances pleasure and brings new perspectives to our daily life. Claus Riedel once found some very clear words for his views on design. His comments make his fascinating purism comprehensible and they also demonstrate how thoroughly he situates his notions of design in a cultural context. They are recorded some passages from a speech he held on various occasions on »The Design of Drinking Glasses Yesterday, Today, Tomorrow«:

Today, I'm speaking to you about glass design, as both a designer myself and as an industrialist and seller [...] What does design mean to us? Rectangular lines? Round balls? Cones turned on their tips? Cylindrical, colored wine glasses?

No, ladies and gentlemen! Design means a package – a composition – the artistic idea complemented with: First, knowledge of the material; second, knowledge of crafting; third, knowledge of function; fourth, the awareness of the cultural sphere in which the object is to be used.

Naturally, resulting from all that is also the price.

For example, if I get a commission from a French crystal factory to create a flower vase, I must be aware that for a dinner invitation I should bring flowers worth ten French francs.

By the way, right now I can exchange French francs, Swiss francs and Swedish crowns one-to-one. I need to know that in Nice I can get thirty or forty carnations for ten francs, that in Zurich I only get seven or eight carnations for ten Swiss francs and that in Stockholm I get one or two carnations for ten Swedish crowns.

Is it any surprise then that I would design flower vases in one size for France and another size for Switzerland? For Scandinavian countries, though, I'd want to design a flower vase with a lid if possible so that the air in the room doesn't dry out the petals.

So you see how important awareness of an individual cultural sphere is. We're talking about function and need to know that aesthetics alone are not enough for design [...] If, say, you're conceiving a set of china and need to know about the function of a coffee- or teapot, then as a designer of a drinking glass you need a much greater knowledge, knowledge of aromas, for example.

Surely the one or other of you has at one time dropped a perfume bottle that broke then. The perfume that ran out certainly didn't smell very good. But it's a completely different matter with the pleasant scent you get when you dab a very small drop of the perfume on your skin.

The smell of wines works the same

264. 3

Funktion — Aromatik — das Wissen um den Lingualis — das Geschmacksempfinden von Zunge und Gaumen.

erzeugte. So kommt es, dieser Vetrarius stammte aus einer syrischen Schule, daß man auf der Iberischen Halbinsel, im ehemaligen Gallien, im früheren Germanien, aber auch um Vindobona stets die gleichen Glasgefäße und die gleiche Glasmacherkunst gefunden hat.

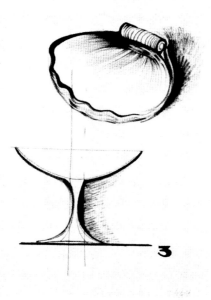

Bild 3

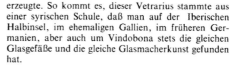

Bild 4

Die Zungenspitze gibt uns die Säuernis des Weines, der Zungenrand die Süße des Weines, der Gaumen und das Zungenende das Salz und die Bitternis.

Und was ist Trinken selbst? Nur die Befriedigung des Durstgefühles oder das Erfreuen der 5 Sinne, die wir mit auf unseren Lebensweg bekommen haben?

Es ist doch so, daß sich das Auge erfreut und prüft und unterscheidet, wenn der goldene Weißwein oder der purpurne Rotwein das Glas füllt. Es ist ein Wohlgefühl für den Tastsinn, wenn wir mit unserer Hand das Glas berühren, um die Temperatur zu prüfen. Wir erfreuen unseren Geruchssinn beim Einatmen vor dem Trinken, wenn wir das Glas mit dem richtigen Volumen auf das Getränk abgestimmt, zum Munde führen um das Bukett zu erahnen. Endlich erfrischen wir die Zunge und schmecken all die Säuernis, all die Süße, all das fruchtige Aroma.

Schon die römischen Cäsaren führten einen Vetrarius mit sich, der ihnen nach der Eroberung eines Landes am neuen Feldherrensitz einen Glasofen aufstellte und gläserne Becher für den Weingenuß

Zwei Becher, die aneinander stoßen, klingen kaum. Die Fertigung eines Kelches war zu diesen Zeiten unbekannt und so kam es, daß ein Vetrarius am Rhein, an einen Becher eine fortlaufende Spirale ansponn. Somit war der Römer gefunden, das Glas, mit dem man, wenn man es geleert hatte, an ein anderes anstieß, um den Mundschenk zu rufen und zu sagen, ich will mehr Wein? Endlich wurde durch den Wohllaut, den dieses Römerglas hervorbrachte, auch der 5. Sinn beim Trinken erfreut.

IV.

Wenn wir bis jetzt rund um das Glas, rund um das Trinkgefäß philosophiert haben, so darf ich Ihnen nun meine Erkenntnisse über die verschiedenen Glasformen mitteilen.

1. das Branntweinglas K 401/5.
Wir erinnern uns an die zerbrochene Parfumflasche und wissen, daß Branntwein sehr edel

264. 2

nalen Beispiel erklären, wie wichtig Funktion für den Designer ist. Nicht etwa, daß man ein Glas so oder so anfaßt, sondern vielleicht sogar das Wissen um die Tee- und um die Kaffeekanne. Die Kaffeekanne wird eine gekochte Flüssigkeit umschließen, aus welcher sich der Kaffeesatz sedimentiert. Deshalb muß eine Kaffeekanne schlank und hoch sein und den Ausguß oben haben, daß ich die klare Flüssigkeit in die Tasse schütten kann.

Wie anders ist das Problem bei der Teekanne. Die trockenen Teeblätter werden eingestreut und die Kanne mit kochendem Wasser angefüllt. Hier muß der Ausguß freilich unten sein, so daß die Teeflüssigkeit jedesmal beim Ausgießen über die aromaspendenden Blätter darüberstreicht.

So duften auch die verlangen deshalb nach lichen Oberflächen zur spiegels.

Schon die alten Ägypt tranken ihren Wein au Kuhhorn, aus dem man zu erfahren, das Kuhho schen von den Schwer eine Fröhlichkeit, die ih

Jenes Kuhhorn, das Triumphe feiert.

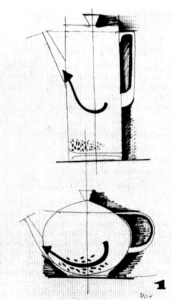

Bild 1

Wenn man als Entwerfer für ein Porzellangeschirr um die Funktion der Kaffee- und der Teekanne wissen muß, so muß man als Designer für ein Trinkglas ein viel größeres Wissen haben, ein Wissen z.B. über die Aromatik. Sicher ist dem einen oder anderen von Ihnen schon einmal ein Parfumfläschchen heruntergefallen und dabei kaputtgegangen. Dieses ausgeronnene Parfum hat gewiss keinen Wohlgeruch verbreitet. Ganz anders aber verhält es sich mit dem Wohlgeruch, wenn Sie einen Tropfen Parfum auf Ihre Haut aufbringen und diesen dort verdunsten lassen.

Aber die alten Ägypt edlen Rebensaft, sonde zu brennen. Dieser We einer Muschelschale ges

Nun, meine Damen gewiß noch an die flach ters Vitrine. Aus diesen nen, wie eng das Pro Verschiedenheit des T

previous page: The credo of Claus Riedel: Wines and champagnes smell differently and therefore require drinking glasses with different surfaces

right: A designer has to follow his nose: When designing coffee pots or wine glasses, it is essential to know about the aroma development of the products

264. 7

n Weine und
nit unterschied-
es Flüssigkeits-

n Weinbau und
horn, Dasselbe
Glückseligkeit
ktar die Men-
s emporhob in
ng gab.

Füllhorn seine

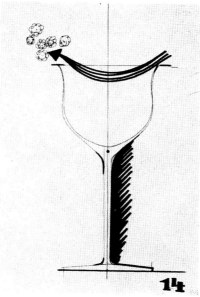

Bild 14

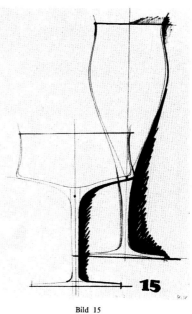

Bild 15

2

nur um den
ch den Wein
damals mittels
hlürft.

erinnern sich
in Großmut-
gen Sie erken-
uß » und die
mmenhängen.

way and therefore requires drinking glasses with various surfaces and liquid levels.

The ancient Egyptians already knew winemaking and drank their wine from a cow's horn, the horn they drank from to feel pleasure, the horn whose nectar raised them from the troubles of the day to a level of happiness that gave them fulfillment.

It is that same horn that has survived to today as a cornucopia.

But the ancient Egyptians didn't just know about wine. They also knew a lot about how to distill it. In those days the brandy these people produced was ladled up with a clamshell and then happily slurped out of it.

Now, ladies and gentlemen! You can surely recall the flat liqueur bowls in Grandma's cabinet. With these two examples you may recognize how intricately the problem of »wine enjoyment« is connected to the range of different drinking glasses.

The tip of the tongue gives us the sweetness and the edges give us the sourness of the wine, while the palate and the back of the tongue tell us its saltiness and bitterness.

And what is drinking itself? Just the quenching of thirst or perhaps the great pleasure of the five senses life has so very kindly granted us?

It's a fact that the eye delights and probes and discerns when a golden white wine or a purple red wine fills a glass.

It is a pleasure to the touch when our hand grasps the glass to test its temperature.

We please our sense of smell by inhaling before we drink, when we raise the glass to our lips, its volume matched perfectly to the drink, and get a waft of the bouquet.

At last we refresh the tongue and taste all the acidity, all the sweetness, all that fruity aroma.

Even the ancient Roman Caesars brought a Vetrarius along so that, in lately conquered lands, he would set up a glass furnace on the new imperial manor and make glass cups for wine. And, since this man came from a Syrian school, this is why we're always finding the same glass vessels and the same glassmaking art on the Iberian Peninsula, in former Gaul, in former Germania and even in Vindobona.

Now, two cups knocked together would hardly make any kind of ringing sound. Making a wineglass bowl was unknown then, and thus it came to pass one day that a Vetrarius on the Rhine added a spiral base to a cup. The *Römer* was born, the glass that, once emptied, you could knock against another to ring out to the man at the tap for more wine.

At last, with this pleasant tone from the *Römer* glass, drinking gave the fifth sense something to be happy about […]

With this lecture, I really want to impress upon you how important it is when designing a form not only to pay lots of attention to aesthetics, the artistic idea. You also need to possess an extensive knowledge of the product's material in order to create a quality article that you can ultimately call beautiful.

Legendary Riedel Handcrafting:
As Smooth and Effortless as Ballet

Claus Riedel had found the core concept, creating the basis for a completely new philosophy of stemware, which has since been developed further by his son Georg. As a result, the production of Riedel glasses today is state of the art, based on a 2,000-year-old handicraft tradition. The hand-made Riedel crystal glass is the queen among glasses. Georg Riedel describes its production to his customers as follows:

Since 1986 Riedel has used electric furnaces for environmental reasons. The furnaces are built out of heat-resistant materials and have clay or ceramic crucibles in which raw materials are melted down into molten crystal. This kind of furnace is used to manufacture handmade, mouth-blown glass. Machined glass is made in melting tanks with a constant glass flow.

The crucible contains a 70 percent glass mix: A mixture of quartz sand, lead oxide, sodium and potassium. To improve the melting qualities of the mixture, the other 30 percent is cullet, raw or broken glass. The melting process takes about eight hours. This requires temperatures of over 1,400 degrees Celsius in order to turn this mixture into liquid crystal glass and cleans it of minor impurities (like gas that might cause tiny bubbles).

The glass takes three hours to cool down. The melting temperature is gently reduced to 1,100 degrees, giving the glass the perfect viscosity for further working by our master glass-blowers.

In our Austrian glass factories the same traditional glass blowing technique is used as 2,000 years ago. Five glassmakers work together in a team. The master blower and his assistant, the so-called »gatherer«, are responsible for the bowl, the top part of the glass. The »gaffer« and his two assistants, the »servitor« and the »bit gatherer«, do the stem and foot.

Work proceeds smoothly. When you watch the glassmakers at work in front of a roaring furnace, it looks like ballet. Each step and each move is precise and rhythmic. The team follows the gaffer. He sets the pace. He determines the work speed and thus also how many handmade pieces are produced in an hour. That is what the team's pay is based on.

The production of the stemmed glass begins: The gatherer pulls a »gather«, a wad of molten glass, from the furnace. With his mouth, he blows a small bubble called a »parison«. For this he uses a 160 cm long, stainless steel tube. It is called a »blowpipe« and has a mouthpiece at one end, and the glass is placed on the other end. The 1,100-degree glass has a viscosity comparable to honey.

Second step: The glass blower – a craftsman

Only with strong lungs are glasses of the highest perfection to be made

with years of experience and the second-most important member of the team – takes over the pipe from the »gatherer«, goes to the furnace with the slightly cooled parison, and dips it into the molten glass until he has exactly the weight he needs for the object being made. The blower has to keep the blowpipe in motion at all times. The yellow-glowing molten glass must be constantly spun and turned so that it does not drip.

Glassmakers usually work with their bare hands, cold water and simple wooden tools. The »block« is used to pre-form and perfectly distribute the glass. This is necessary for the next step. The pre-formed glass at the end of the pipe is now ready to be shaped. A mold is used to create the object's shape and size. To absorb moisture, molds are made of either hardwood (pear wood) or aluminum with a graphite surface. The glass blower uses his breath, blowing carefully into the pipe to fill the mold. The bowl never touches the mold because the moisture begins to form steam. A steam »cushion« protects the sensitive glass surface primarily from spots and scratches. This step produces a bowl with a lid that must be removed later.

The »servitor«, the assistant to the gaffer – passes the pipe with the finished bowl to him. The gaffer is now in charge of the stem and the foot. The next stage of production begins with a gather of molten glass. The »bit gatherer« (second assistant) uses his pipe to give the gather to the gaffer. He cuts it with special shears and affixes it on the bowl. The exact size and weight are the keys to quality. The gaffer pulls the molten glass by hand with simple tools into a thin stem of exact length and correct thickness.

The foot begins as another gather affixed to the stem. The »bit gatherer« again uses his pipe to give the gather to the gaffer so that he can form the foot, or footplate. The gaffer uses a »clapper« and cold water, bringing the foot by hand into the exact shape and thickness.

This work requires years of training, a passion for precision, a sure hand, a very good eye and exceptional hand-eye coordination.

The glass must be cooled carefully to avoid

A sure hand, a good eye and years of training make one a master. Only flawless glasses receive the Riedel seal of quality

stress cracks that can be caused by the transformation of the quartz. As it cools from 1,100 degrees Celsius to room temperature, the glass shrinks.

To prevent stress cracks, we use a »lehr« or cooling oven. It looks like a tunnel and has different temperature zones. The glass moves along a steel conveyor belt and cools down from 450 degrees to room temperature. As the glass is very thin-blown, this takes about 2.5 hours.

The careful working of the rim that makes contact with our lips is important. The final working of the stem glass goes like this: The lid is broken off the bowl and the rim is very carefully cut. Then the glass is washed and polished until it is absolutely perfect. These final steps ensure our delight when the rim touches our lips.

Experts with years of experience conduct the quality control. The glass is optically examined, and only flawless, completely clear glasses pass this inspection. The glasses are weighed to guarantee that they are within their range of acceptability.

Only glasses that have passed this quality control can bear the Riedel logo, a sand-engraved signature.

The manually made Riedel crystal glass is the queen of glasses – the glassmakers at Riedel Glass know it

Riedel Crystal 2006:
Two Generations Face a Promising Future

The tenth and eleventh Riedel generation, Georg Riedel and his son Maximilian: The history of this family continues to be written. Glass has always been the passion of this dynastic company, but each generation met different challenges that had to be dealt with and mastered. Each generation faced economic, political, social and cultural conditions that offered enormous opportunities, but also bore risks. The opportunities were seen and seized, and the risks were overcome sometimes with smaller and sometimes with larger losses. Through it all, the individual members of the dynasty followed one idea: Upholding a tradition.

Many businessmen like to portray themselves as going from rags to riches, fabulous riches even. Such stories with their predictable superlatives are eagerly snapped up by the press as filler material. The Riedels are far from exposing themselves to the media on this level. Their corporate philosophy focuses on understatement. Which does not mean they are not proud and self-confident. It is just that excessive extravagance is not in the family's nature. Georg Riedel simply says, »What is there to write about my life anyway?«

Appellations like »the Glass King« or »industry magnate«, that were once given to some of their ancestors, are not what make this dynasty fascinating. It's something else. It is the remarkably long view this family takes, the goals and values that have remained the same for over a quarter of a millennium and have been almost stoically followed and courageously lived out. It is this sense of obligation to want to keep creating in the future. If we take a close look at the various personalities who have led the company through all its crises and successes, then it seems almost as though the family had been formed from a single drop of molten glass – as though it constituted one single work of art made from the glass they gave their lives to.

It will not be any easier for the generations to follow to add further to this work of art. Every decade makes it more impressive, splendid – and obligating. Johann Christoph Riedel, happily whistling as he wheeled along his pushcart loaded with glass to sell his wares in different towns, was free from tradition and the responsibilities that grew from it. Glass King Josef Riedel, on the other hand, the sixth in the line, already had forefathers who were entrepreneurial role models. Georg Riedel and his son Maximilian are currently right in the middle of this exemplary entrepreneurial saga with quite a legacy to bear. They don´t wish to be the last, they cannot give up, or sell out, or fail in any way.

2006 is an anniversary year, 250 years of Riedel. If one looks back, it is continuity that one notices. And a great variety of talents, be they business, technical or artistic. Their interaction has created a unique composition, unlike any other family business.

The tenth and eleventh generations face what may be an especially great challenge, perhaps the

The 10th and 11th generation of Riedels: Georg Riedel (born 1949) with his son Maximilian (born 1977) and his daughter Laetizia (born 1974)

greatest of all. In a world of global corporate structures, production sites are treated like transfer depots where a succession of managers are used as fodder to turn up the heat, a family business of this size – a mid-sized company – feels almost exotic. But the great strength of each Riedel has always been the strategy of the karate fighter. Do not wait for the opponent to act, but anticipate what is coming.

Georg Riedel, commemorating the jubilee year 2006 as the tenth in the line, demonstrates tremendous skill in this area. Among his special talents is the strategic long-term view. Failure would be the ultimate catastrophe for him, but the thought of it drives him to ever higher achievements. When he goes into meetings, he thinks in large dimensions, not of the numbers after the decimal point but of round numbers. Always extremely well prepared, he knows exactly what will come from the other side of the table and how he will react to it.

He has the edge in more than just meetings. He reacts to market developments before most people even recognize them. In the fall of 2004 Georg Riedel used previously saved capital to buy the German glass company F. X. Nachtmann AG, which was far larger in terms of personnel and output (six production sites in all), but running at a loss. Georg Riedel: »The situation at that company had been acute.« One might assume that this was a company blindly acquiring an economically weak subsidiary, convinced that expansion would bring higher profits. This was not the case. With this apparently unusual step Riedel was following a clear concept: Whereas up to then Riedel had been organized around the manufacture of wine and spirits glasses – which of course, will remain the case – it was important to avoid in advance potential dead ends. Handmade glasses for fine wines will always find their buyers, but their production is extremely expensive. At the same time, machine-made glasses have made huge progress. Today it is possible to mass-produce glasses even for the gourmet sector, glasses so fine and perfect that a wine connoisseur has no complaints. However, Georg Riedel did not decide to take over Nachtmann simply with regard to creating a broader base of industrial production, but rather as a strategic move designed to further strengthen the US business which in 2005 represents 40 percent of sales.

For the distribution of Riedel products in America, Georg Riedel set up the company Riedel Crystal of America in 1979. His son Maximilian currently works there as CEO, while his daughter Laetizia is the Riedel in-house lawyer. Maximilian Riedel has already written a chapter in the Riedel success story: He initiated the »O« series introduced in 2004 – stemless wine glasses of the finest Riedel quality. This line of glasses quickly became a surprise success, particularly popular among American and Japanese wine drinkers.

What Claus Riedel initiated with his legendary Sommeliers series, Georg Riedel is bringing to perfection. There are all kinds of wine glasses available, but there is still only *one* Riedel wine glass. More than ever, Riedel wine glasses distinguish themselves through their evolution, beginning with the Sommeliers series created by Claus Riedel (9) and further developing since 1982 under Georg Riedel (10), as uncompromising grape-specific glasses. When one drinks wine from them, one can truly envisage that sun-baked vineyard. In a time in which the location, the specific wine region, no longer plays the major role, in which winemakers have been intensively creating hybrid wines with great experimental glee, correctly matching wine to a wine glass requires careful consideration.

In the face of the increasing perfection of machine-made glasses, the market presence of handmade glasses will recede. But they will always be a part of Riedel as long as there are gourmets who refuse to do without them.

In the future, the three glass brands – Riedel, Spiegelau and Nachtmann – will be clearly positioned without any overlap, with Riedel remaining the name that targets wine connoisseurs and the most demanding customers. In the spirit of »quality made in Europe« Georg Riedel is creating the foundation of a new corporate constellation. He knows well that his family's past is impressive – and

Georg Riedel and his wife Eva – a power couple

the future needs to be tackled. Riedel Crystal: Synonymous for years with wine and spirits glasses of exceptional quality and timeless design that deliver maximum drinking pleasure. It will stay that way.

Its excellent image this anniversary year now comes hand-in-hand with a position as the world's largest glass company. The Riedel Company has created a springboard for penetrating further the world's markets.

And is now poised for another leap.

Brought to perfection: The Sommeliers series (here for red wines) has been further developed by Georg Riedel to create grape-specific glasses

Appendix

Eleven Generations
The Riedel Dynasty at a Glance

The first
JOHANN CHRISTOPH RIEDEL
(1673–1744)

The second
JOHANN CARL RIEDEL
(1701–1781)

The fourth
ANTON LEOPOLD RIEDEL
(1761–1821)

JOS

The third
JOHANN LEOPOLD RIEDEL
(1726–1800)

The fifth
FRANZ XAVER ANTON RIEDEL
(1786–1844)

JOS

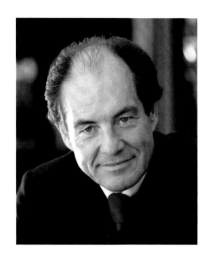

The eighth
WALTER RIEDEL
(1895–1974)

The tenth
GEORG JOSEF RIEDEL
(born 1949)

The ninth
CLAUS JOSEF RIEDEL
(1925–2004)

The eleventh
MAXIMILIAN RIEDEL
(born 1977)

...nior

...nior

The Riedel Family Tree

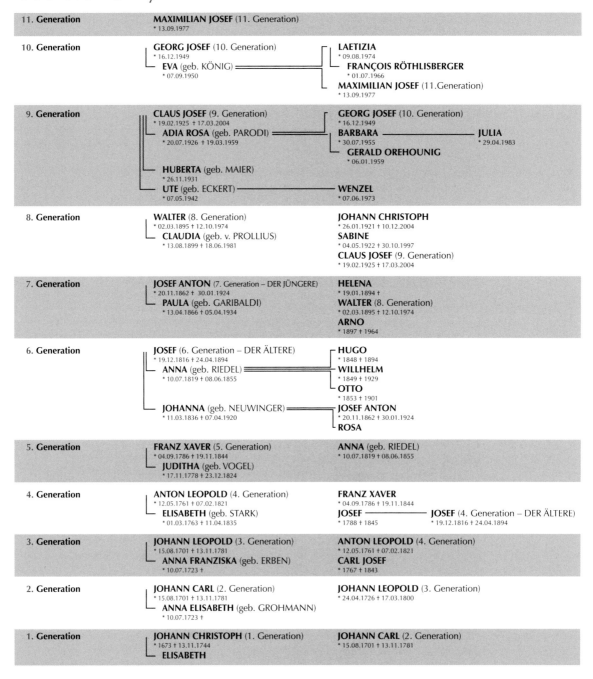

11. Generation　　**MAXIMILIAN JOSEF** (11. Generation)
　　* 13.09.1977

10. Generation　　**GEORG JOSEF** (10. Generation)　　**LAETIZIA**
　　* 16.12.1949　　* 09.08.1974
　　EVA (geb. KÖNIG)　　**FRANÇOIS RÖTHLISBERGER**
　　* 07.09.1950　　* 01.07.1966
　　　　MAXIMILIAN JOSEF (11.Generation)
　　　　* 13.09.1977

9. Generation　　**CLAUS JOSEF** (9. Generation)　　**GEORG JOSEF** (10. Generation)
　　* 19.02.1925 † 17.03.2004　　* 16.12.1949
　　ADIA ROSA (geb. PARODI)　　**BARBARA** —————————— **JULIA**
　　* 20.07.1926 † 19.03.1959　　* 30.07.1955　　* 29.04.1983
　　　　GERALD OREHOUNIG
　　　　* 06.01.1959
　　HUBERTA (geb. MAIER)
　　* 26.11.1931
　　UTE (geb. ECKERT) ———————————— **WENZEL**
　　* 07.05.1942　　* 07.06.1973

8. Generation　　**WALTER** (8. Generation)　　**JOHANN CHRISTOPH**
　　* 02.03.1895 † 12.10.1974　　* 26.01.1921 † 10.12.2004
　　CLAUDIA (geb. v. PROLLIUS)　　**SABINE**
　　* 13.08.1899 † 18.06.1981　　* 04.05.1922 † 30.10.1997
　　　　CLAUS JOSEF (9. Generation)
　　　　* 19.02.1925 † 17.03.2004

7. Generation　　**JOSEF ANTON** (7. Generation – DER JÜNGERE)　　**HELENA**
　　* 20.11.1862 † 30.01.1924　　* 19.01.1894 †
　　PAULA (geb. GARIBALDI)　　**WALTER** (8. Generation)
　　* 13.04.1866 † 05.04.1934　　* 02.03.1895 † 12.10.1974
　　　　ARNO
　　　　* 1897 † 1964

6. Generation　　**JOSEF** (6. Generation – DER ÄLTERE)　　**HUGO**
　　* 19.12.1816 † 24.04.1894　　* 1848 † 1894
　　ANNA (geb. RIEDEL)　　**WILLHELM**
　　* 10.07.1819 † 08.06.1855　　* 1849 † 1929
　　　　OTTO
　　　　* 1853 † 1901
　　JOHANNA (geb. NEUWINGER)　　**JOSEF ANTON**
　　* 11.03.1836 † 07.04.1920　　* 20.11.1862 † 30.01.1924
　　　　ROSA

5. Generation　　**FRANZ XAVER** (5. Generation)　　**ANNA** (geb. RIEDEL)
　　* 04.09.1786 † 19.11.1844　　* 10.07.1819 † 08.06.1855
　　JUDITHA (geb. VOGEL)
　　* 17.11.1778 † 23.12.1824

4. Generation　　**ANTON LEOPOLD** (4. Generation)　　**FRANZ XAVER**
　　* 12.05.1761 † 07.02.1821　　* 04.09.1786 † 19.11.1844
　　ELISABETH (geb. STARK)　　**JOSEF** ——————— **JOSEF** (4. Generation – DER ÄLTERE)
　　* 01.03.1763 † 11.04.1835　　* 1788 † 1845　　* 19.12.1816 † 24.04.1894

3. Generation　　**JOHANN LEOPOLD** (3. Generation)　　**ANTON LEOPOLD** (4. Generation)
　　* 15.08.1701 † 13.11.1781　　* 12.05.1761 † 07.02.1821
　　ANNA FRANZISKA (geb. ERBEN)　　**CARL JOSEF**
　　* 10.07.1723 †　　* 1767 † 1843

2. Generation　　**JOHANN CARL** (2. Generation)　　**JOHANN LEOPOLD** (3. Generation)
　　* 15.08.1701 † 13.11.1781　　* 24.04.1726 † 17.03.1800
　　ANNA ELISABETH (geb. GROHMANN)
　　* 10.07.1723 †

1. Generation　　**JOHANN CHRISTOPH** (1. Generation)　　**JOHANN CARL** (2. Generation)
　　* 1673 † 13.11.1744　　* 15.08.1701 † 13.11.1781
　　ELISABETH

Map of the Riedel Glassworks

Brief Connoisseur's Guide

The finest glasses for both technical and hedonistic purposes are those made by Riedel. The effect of these glasses on fine wine is profound. I cannot emphasize enough what a difference they make.

Robert M. Parker, Jr. – The Wine Advocate

I. A fine wine demands a fine glass

In 1973 in Orvieto, with the cooperation of the Italian Association of Sommeliers (ASI), Claus J. Riedel unveiled »Sommeliers«, the first gourmet glass series in the world, encompassing ten different sizes at that time.

Since then, the world of wine has changed profoundly. Today, wines come from regions and continents that were inconceivable back then.

Along with this development, the Sommeliers range has grown into a comprehensive, state-of-the-art »vitrum-vinotheque« and has risen to become the most successful handmade glass series in the world.

Of course, a glass alone cannot work miracles – the quality of the wine is always the basis and prerequisite. However, it is a fine glass that allows a fine wine truly to unfold its secrets.

Essential basics:

- A colorless, undecorated glass is needed in order to appreciate a wine visually and assess its color, clarity and consistency.
- A thin-blown bowl means the temperature is immediately felt.
- Thick walls have the disadvantage of transferring the temperature of the glass to the drink.
- Swirling wine in the glass heightens the pleasure of the bouquet.
- Enlarging the evaporation surface area increases the variety and intensity of aromas.
- Scents are best experienced by bringing the nose into the correct position from which it can search for the message of the wine deep in the center of the glass.

Now we are ready for the first drink – bearing in mind that wine is drunk »in sips«. Each wine requires its own form of wineglass in order to unfold fully.

The size and shape of a glass provide the basic information for the posture of the body, whereas the diameter of the rim determines the position of the head. The latest ultrasound studies have shown that the tongue also takes up different positions depending on the form and shape of the glass. The lips are first to sense the nature of the rim and the thickness of the glass.

II. Pleasure in every sense

Sight: The first contact with the wine. It registers things like a wine's color, but also the visual effect of the glass.

Touch: A Riedel glass should always be picked up by the stem. Feel the perfect balance of the glass. Handcrafting guarantees the silken surface of the stem, foot and bowl.

Smell: In order not to falsify the characteristics of the wine, it is necessary to match the form and vol-

1   2   3   4   5   6

1 This balloon glass with a rolled rim makes every wine short and sour.

2 For fruity, light white wines of high acidity. This form accentuates the fruit with a bittersweet aftertaste – ideal for rieslings.

3 For full-bodied, strong white wines of moderate acidity. This form accentuates the acid and deemphasizes the alcohol – ideal for chardonnay.

4 For champagne. This form highlights the bouquet and the fine pearling.

5 For heavy red wines with high acid and medium tannin. This form celebrates the fruit and represses the acid – ideal for pinot noir. The cut rim allows the wine to flow smoothly onto the tongue.

6 For highly tannic heavy red wines of medium acidity. This form brings out the fruit and represses the tannin – ideal for cabernet-sauvignon. The cut rim allows the wine to flow smoothly onto the tongue.

ume of the glass to the character of a drink. The intensity of aromas is increased by swirling the glass. The quality of a fine wine is particularly present in its bouquet. Take a conscious pleasure in this experience.

Taste: The form of the glass, its volume and the diameter of the rim direct the sip of wine onto the tongue. With its tactile sense, we are able to register the temperature and consistency of the wine before it further unfolds on the palate. The taste intensities of fruit, acid and tannin are expressed completely differently in different glass forms. Even the finish is heavily influenced by the form of the glass. The right glass leaves the mouth with a pleasant memory, eagerly awaiting the next sip.

Hearing: Glasses can't speak. But they do sound wonderful when you touch glasses to make a toast. Make sure you don't touch glasses at the rim or the foot, but rather at the widest point (»cheek to cheek«).

»Tongue map«: The tongue is covered with variously formed papillae that make its surface appear rough. Most of them, however, are filiform papillae that contain no taste buds. The fungiform papillae are mainly concentrated around the tip of the tongue, which contributes over-proportionately to the sense of taste, and on the sides of the tongue. The wrinkly foliate papillae are located on the rear sides, and finally the vallate papillae are larger, wall-like structures around the base of the tongue.

III. Tasting wine – a brief anatomical guide to flavor

Controlled by the form and rim, a sip of fifteen to twenty milligrams moistens an exactly determined area of the mouth. The viscosity and temperature of the drink are transmitted by touch. Shortly after that the taste begins to develop. The tongue and its taste receptors can distinguish only four sensations, sweet at the tip, bitter in the back, and saltiness and sourness on the sides.

Depending on the form, size and rim diameter of a glass, the body, head and tongue take up a specific position. Thus, it becomes possible to position a sip exactly in order to activate specific taste buds.

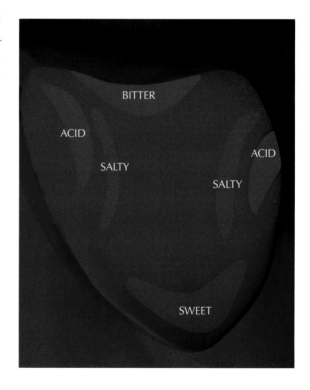

The intensive, multifaceted flavor sensations, however, only emerge in combination with the bouquet. The mouth is connected to the nose through the throat, so we smell and taste at the same time. Fruit, acid, tannin and alcohol are the variable flavor components of a wine that a glass transmits.

As an instrument of drinking pleasure, the glass is responsible for the harmony and balance of these components. When tasting wines, whether dry or sweet, the interplay of fruit and acid on the tongue is very important. With the right glass, they can be harmoniously attuned to each other.

IV. Perfect pleasure – a very special experience

Swallowing the wine immediately would reduce the pleasure. For this reason, wine is swirled around the mouth to address all the flavor receptors. Some people pucker their lips to experience the flavor more intensively.

Finally, swallowing and the finish the wine leaves determine quality and enjoyment. In this way, the bitterness of a highly tannic red wine can be experienced differently through the glass transmitter: In different glasses, the flavor profile of the same wine can emerge anywhere from pleasantly round and fruity to vegetal, harsh and astringent. Even the wine's aftertaste on the palate is the result of complex mechanisms of the body that are determined by the glass's form.

A fine wine becomes a perfect pleasure only through the glass in which it is served.

Register

Picture Credits

Cover picture: Riedel-Glas, Kufstein

Photos: FinePic p. 184, p. 185; Isergebirgs-Museum, Neugablonz p. 10 u. p. 11 above, p. 12, p. 13–15 above, p. 46, p. 51, p. 52, p. 81, p. 83, p. 84, p. 93, p. 126, p. 127, p. 133, p. 148, p. 154; picture-alliance/akg-images p. 19, p. 21, p. 28, p. 31/dpa p. 77, p. 143; Riedel-Glas, Kufstein p. 2–9 oben, p. 14, p. 16, p. 18–22 oben, p. 23, p. 24–29 above, p. 30, p. 31 above, p. 32–36, p. 37–39 oben, p. 40–45, p. 46 u. p. 47 above, p. 48, p. 50–54 above, p. 55–64, p. 65 above, p. 66–76, p. 77–79 above, p. 80, p. 81–84 above, p. 85–92, p. 93 above, p. 94–104, p. 105–111 above, p. 112–125, p. 126–138 oben, p. 139, p. 140–149 above, p. 150–153, p. 154 above, p. 155–168, p. 169 above, p. 170–183, p. 184 u. p. 185 above, p. 186–191, Anhang; The National Museum of Denmark, Ethnographic Collection p. 25; Ullstein/akg Pressebild p. 105/Archiv Gerstenberg p. 39/Dietrich p. 11/ Granger Collection p. 27, p. 37, p. 78/Lombard p. 65/NASA p. 169/SV-Bilderdienst p. 137/ullstein-bild p. 20, p. 110, p. 128, p. 145, p. 147/Weychardt p. 109.